Women and the Labyrinth Theory: Myths and Realities at the

Corporate Level

Pittsburgh, Pennsylvania

Reverend Dr. Deborah A. Harris

Second Edition

ISBN-13: 978-1499647273
ISBN-10: 1499647271
LCCN: 2015906438
BISAC: Business & Economics / General

Abstract

The exploration of this qualitative study sought to comprehend the experiences of 15 women leaders who occupied or sought to occupy upper-level leadership roles in culturally male-dominated corporate offices within Pittsburgh, Pennsylvania. This examination of women in Pittsburgh, Pennsylvania investigated difficulties encountered in the corporate arena as a result of barriers known as Labyrinthine phenomenon. The Labyrinth phenomenon is a metaphor symbolizing the complexities that hinder the paths (for women in the case of this study) to leadership (Eagly & Carli (2007). The labyrinth contains numerous ever-changing barriers, some subtle, unexpected, tortious, and otherwise blatantly obvious road blocks. Eagly and Carli (2007 and Eagly and Sczesny (2009) suggested the labyrinth is indicative of the numerous barriers and paths women encounter as they aspire leadership position in corporate offices. This phenomenon becomes complex by life events (education, family obligations, etc.,) associated with labyrinth phenomenon. The specific problem regarding the labyrinthine phenomenon presents tortious twisting paths that complicate and interfere with women's advancement to the corporate suite. Six main themes emerged treatment by industry standards, gender bias, work-life challenges, success determinants, emotions, leadership roles, and the labyrinthine phenomenon. Five subthemes were identified family obligations, gender bias, stress, loneliness, and the labyrinth phenomenon. Finding from the themes identified characteristics of gender bias (a) dismissive behavior toward women in leadership roles, (b) precarious leadership roles, (c) double standards of family obligation, and (d) refusal to integrate the work-life leadership models.

Dedication

This is dedicated to God who made a way out of no way; whose word says He has an expected and successful end for us. God opened doors and made a way that no man could have done. He sustained my heart, mind, and spirit through some incredibly difficult times, made connections, and provided amazing support systems throughout this awesome journey.

I also dedicate this to my husband, Reverend Louis Harris, and son, Christopher Shields, who unconditionally supported the dream of this journey. I love you and thank them for their patience along the way; I could not have done this without them cheering me on. Louis, Chris; prayers alone were felt every day and greatly appreciated. The love you both showered upon me, especially when things were difficult was incredible. I, especially appreciate those crazy moments of levity you both casted upon me when you saw the stress levels rising. They were priceless mind saving moments. What is more appreciated was, the insistence that I take the time to laugh at some crazy video clip, when I was in the deepest thought, totally energized, made way for a fresh perspective and inspired every step of my journey. Thank you!

Table of Contents

Chapter 1: Introduction

The glass ceiling metaphor (Bendl & Schmidt, 2010) indicates that women have not advanced in corporate offices within the United States because of an invisible barrier or barriers imposed to hinder women's approach to executive management. Bendl and Schmidt (2010) proposed that though women have made significant strides in obtaining, roles of leadership the progress remains slow and women continue to encounter obstacles that hinder their ascent to leadership. Haney (2010) postulated that only 15 of the Fortune 500 companies have women as chief executive officers (CEOs), and on average, full-time female workers make 23% less than full-time male workers (Catalyst, 2008; Haney, 2010). Bias and discrimination continue to slow or totally block the advancement of women in corporate offices, in the United States; the dominant issues associated to the paths taken by women in their attempt to ascend the corporate ladder. Eagly and Carli (2007) posited that an examination of the difficulties women encountered from the paths, such as education, and family responsibilities, and so forth; women take present a different metaphor that they refer to as labyrinth.

The purpose of the current investigation was to develop an understanding of the labyrinth experiences women encounter while attempting to advance in executive leadership (e.g., cracking the glass ceiling). Eagly and Carli (2007) proposed instead of the unyielding glass ceiling, a labyrinth is an unrestricted and open-ended maze of events that hinders the ability some women to navigate successfully the corporate ladder.

A labyrinth begins to form as women strategically maneuver between continuing discrimination, family responsibilities, and stereotypical bigotry. Eagly and Carli (2007) further contended some women successfully maneuver these obstacles and find their way through the labyrinth and reach executive offices. The goal of the investigation was to provide comprehension of the working conditions within Pittsburgh, Pennsylvania, corporate offices, and explain the conditions presented by the labyrinthine theory have become the new glass ceiling for women in the Pittsburgh corporate arena.

Chapter 1 includes a synopsis of the current investigation and conditions that affect women working to pursue upper-level leadership roles in corporate offices. An examination of the investigative premise may provide comprehension of current working environment, the significance, and specific problems, encountered in this purposed labyrinthine premise.

Background of the Problem

Hymowitz and Schellhardt (1986), focusing on women in corporate offices, first expressed the glass ceiling metaphor in a *Wall Street Journal* report. The authors presented the glass ceiling metaphor in reference to the barriers faced as women aspired to attain senior executive positions. The use of the glass ceiling metaphor is no longer applicable as leaders becomes aware of the labyrinthine theory that affects every leadership environments, corporations, educational facilities, governments, and nonprofit organizations nationally and internationally.

Eagly (2007) introduced the labyrinth metaphor as dissimilarity to the glass ceiling metaphor addressing the continuing barriers women encounter as they aspire to reach executive positions from a different perspective. The obstacles of the labyrinth metaphor discussed by Eagly focused on how women drift off track because of various turns in life such as family, financial issues, personal choices, and discrimination. According to Eagly and Carli (2007), as presented by Santovec (2007), the labyrinth represents a continual set of obstacles women stumble upon in their pursuit of executive leadership. The labyrinth phenomenon starts at the beginning of a woman's career and begin to form with every twisting obstacle encountered in her pursuit to the executive suite.

However, the glass ceiling theory may be associated to women seeking promotion into upper leadership positions the experiences of encountered by the labyrinthine phenomenon presents an entirely different scenario of difficulties women encounter as they attempt to ascend the corporate ladder (Mathur & Chadha, 2010). Mathur and Chadha (2010) proposed the glass ceiling theory describes the social economic disparities that between women and men in senior leadership positions that do not address the expanse of the labyrinthine effects on women leaders. Eagly and Carli (2007) and Hansen (2009) suggested the glass ceiling phenomenon existed and imposed barriers although women are capable, are exceedingly educated, and able to assume leadership positions disparities continue to exist in corporate America. However, the premise of the labyrinth metaphor acknowledges obstacles and is not ultimately discouraging. As women gain comprehension of the ever-changing twist and turns of the labyrinthine phenomenon, they can navigate their way around them, effectively to improving their situation.

Statement of the Problem

The problem is women in corporate offices in the United States have achieved degrees and certifications but still face issues of discrimination in the corporate arena. According to a Catalyst (2008) report, the gender gap in senior leadership is persistent, and the underrepresented of women in top corporate leadership positions continues. Most large corporations in the United States have made scant progress in advancing women, especially to leadership and top-paying positions over the last decade (Catalyst, 2008).

Women representation across the general workforce is growing; however, there remains a need for information about the challenges women face while attempting to advance their careers (GAO, 2010). The number of women in upper management is less than in the general workforce. In four of the 10 industries reviewed by personnel in the U.S. Government Accounting Office, differences were found in the characteristics and pay of male and female.

The specific problem is that ever-changing barriers known as labyrinthine phenomenon becomes complex by life events or tortious twists associated with labyrinth phenomenon. This labyrinthine phenomenon's hinders a woman's progress from attaining positions of leadership in Pittsburgh's corporate arena. These life events refer to the labyrinthine twisting paths that complicate and interfere with women's advancement to the corporate suite (Okafor & Amalu, 2010). More specifically women who take a path focusing on family responsibilities such as child rearing face major career setbacks when attempting to re-enter corporate America. The labyrinthine phenomenon indicates that women rarely reenter employment at the level of pay or authority when resuming executive pursuits and often lose momentum further hampering their career paths (Eagly & Carli,

2007; 2009; Güngör & Biernat, 2009; Okafor & Amalu, 2010). The intent of the investigation was to explore women's perceptions of the ever-changing labyrinthine paths women navigate in pursuit to executive leadership in Pittsburgh corporate offices.

Purpose of the Investigation

The purpose of this qualitative, phenomenological research was to explore women in executive positions in Pittsburgh corporate offices in relation to the labyrinth phenomenon and their underrepresentation in corporate offices within the United States. Studies conducted by Berry and Franks (2010), Grupta (2009), Heilman and Eagly (2008), Kwolek-Folland (2007), Okafor and Amalu (2010), and Stuhlmacher and Poitras (2010) indicate an understanding of the perceptions associated to the labyrinthine experiences women encounter as it relates to the lack of advancement to executive leadership. The information collected through this investigation provided insight into the labyrinth phenomenon and reasons for why women with equal or extensive backgrounds are not advancing up the corporate ladder.

This phenomenological invesitgation involved face-to-face interviews with employees with various executive levels of women leaders in Pittsburgh based upon participant characteristics, knowledge, and career paths to collect data for the qualitative, phenomenological research. The special consideration of participant characteristics and knowledge was necessary for this investigation (Houghton, Casey, Shaw, & Murphy, 2010). The participants consisted of varying leadership disciplines and roles for women in the Pittsburgh corporate arena.

An examination of the issues of inequality and discrimination related to experiences women in business encounter, known as the labyrinth theory, was the focus of this investigation (Berry & Franks, 2010). The labyrinthine theory remains an unexpected barriers and an obstacle blocking women from executive leadership positions held by male colleagues (Eagly & Carli, 2007; 2010).

This phenomenological investigation involved the arts of asking, witnessing, interpreting, and knowing, which provides an advantage in the collection of data. Collecting data in this manner allowed participant data to be collected without substantially changing the message provided (Barusch, Gringeri, & George, 2011; McQueen et al., 2006). Conducting a qualitative investigative analysis through discussions with the participants was a means to gain understanding of the labyrinthine paths women encounter in their pursuit to executive leadership.

Significance of the Investigation

The significance of this investigation is that it involved exploring and gaining an understanding of women's perspectives of the maze of obstacles that impede the advancement of women into executive leadership positions. Duehr and Bono (2006) and Eagly and Sczesny (2009) speculated as the number of women in management roles increases and organizations place a greater emphasis on diversity, a subsequent change in perceptions of women as leaders occurs. There are three intents of this investigation (a) refutation, (b) thorough analysis of the research topic, and (c) validation of the research premise.

Nature of the Investigation

There are various forms of phenomenological designs (empirical, interpretive, existential, Husserlian, etc.) a researcher can implement to as a foundation of investigation. For example implementing an Interpretive phenomenological analysis (IPA) framework structure for analyzing qualitative research data collected for women in Pittsburgh Pennsylvania's corporate research provided a perspective of the information collected.

According to Grassi (2009), a Husserlian (1938) approach is a form of idealism, aimed toward discovering the ideal form of phenomena, or the essence of expressions. Further, Husserl shares with the idealist a tendency to stress a priori conditions of knowledge (such as with Plato and Kant) "in that it describes and analyzes objective contents of consciousness: ideas, concepts, images, propositions, in short, ideal meanings of various types that serve as intentional contents, or nomadic meanings, of various types of experience" (Grassi, 2009, pp. 90-91). Therefore, the collected data are shareable by different acts of consciousness, and objective in ideal and meanings.

The theoretical foundation of IPA assisted in the comprehension and approach to this investigative research and provided the relevance to his or her particular research questions. IPA allows the analysis of data related to face-to-face one-on-one interviewing in order to develop 'thick descriptions' that may help illuminate human experience. IPA approaches also assists in the development of theories, models, and update policy (Fade, 2004).

The IPA qualitative method was appropriate for this invesitgation, which involved using face-to-face interviews to obtain participant data on women in leadership in the Pittsburgh corporate offices. The method was suitable for exploring the experiences of women's work experiences to review the perceptions on the labyrinth phenomenon that imped their ascent to executive leadership (McQueen & Zimmerman, 2006). The data was analyzed using Moustakas' (1994) modified van Kaam method. The IPA design was an appropriate approach for uncovering the meanings of the participants' daily human experiences. The IPA qualitative, phenomenological approach was also suitable for using an interpretive narrative research approach (McQueen & Zimmerman, 2006) to explore the experiences and suggestions of the participants.

Analyzing the experiences of women in Pittsburgh, Pennsylvania corporate offices regarding the labyrinthine theory led to in-depth insight regarding the phenomenon. The labyrinth relates to a maze of twists and turns created by various life event paths encountered when women suspend corporate pursuits for family responsibilities, educational pursuits. These ongoing mazes and obstacles reflect a different level of discrimination, or sexist stereotypes applicable to women (Eagly & Carli, 2007; Eagly & Sczesny, 2009). The objective of this phenomenological research design was to collect comprehensive data and then analyze the data to identify themes regarding the phenomenon (McQueen & Zimmerman, 2006).

Research Questions

Two research questions guided the foundation of this investigation in exploring labyrinth theories (Leedy & Ormrod, 2010; McQueen et al., 2006; Neuman 2007).

- R1. What barriers do women in corporate offices in Pittsburgh, Pennsylvania, perceive as inhibiting their promotion in the workplace?
- R2. What are the reasons women are leaving corporate offices in Pittsburgh, Pennsylvania, and abandoning the pursuit of executive leadership roles?

The participants provided data that led to answers to the research questions. The participants were business women from the various levels of leadership in Pittsburgh corporate businesses, entrepreneurs from various industries, for profits, and nonprofits organizations. Various criteria were used to recruit individuals who had in-depth experience regarding the phenomenon. The criteria were based partially on the research questions for the investigation (McQueen et al., 2006; Moustakas, 1994; Neuman, 2007). Based on the criteria established enabled the selection of participants, the enabled a data collection process which resulted in valuable information related to the investigative questions.

For example to accomplish the requirements of question two, a thorough examination of the Pittsburgh Businesstimes, Book of lists (PBBL), (2012) provided access to an extensive list of public and private companies owned and operated by women in Pittsburgh, Pennsylvania. Further examination of the PBBL presented a list of the top ranking companies, the entrepreneurial endeavor of each company, level of business networking and competitive landscape listed within a supplement entitled Business Women First.

Also within these publications, readers have access to active forums that speak to or address issues women have or are currently encountering. Additionally, an extensive pool of information of women in various stages of their professional careers is available. These stages represent women actively in leadership roles, women who have stepped down to pursue life events such as educational advancements, family obligations inclusive of but not limited to maternity leave, child and parental care, to health related issues. Having access to this information provided an opportunity to enlist prospective participants to participate in the investigation and presented 60 % of perspective participants. A simple plea to various business forums and offices inquiring an interest in participating in a life event inquiry provided the balance needed to conduct this investigation.

Theoretical Framework

Three theories: conflict theory, role congruity theory and social role theory formed the foundation of this investigative approach. The focus of conflict theory focuses on divergent interests of members of society. Role congruity focuses on the conflicts between an individual's gender role and leadership role. Social role theory relates to spillover effects of gender and social roles in organizations.

Conflict theory. Conflict theory states that society or an organization functions so that each individual participant and its groups struggle to maximize their benefits (Marx circa 1844; Yukl, 2010). Conflict theory focuses on divergent interests of members of society. It assumes that people act as they do to further their interests and that doing so is sometimes at the expense of the interests of others (Henry 2009; Yukl, 2010). Conflict theory states that society or an organization functions so that each individual participant and its groups struggle to maximize their benefits and assumes that people act as they do to further their interests at the expense of the interests of others (Capretta, Clark & Guangrong 2008; Bennis, 2009 & Yukl, 2010).

Role congruity theory. Role incongruity theory of prejudice regards the incongruence of female leadership and gender roles (Eagly & Karau, 2002; Wolfram, Mohr, & Schyns, 2007). Role congruity theorists argue that "there is a considerable overlap between the male gender role and the leadership role" (Wolfram et al., 2007, p. 21). Masculine attributes or characteristics are closely associated with effective leadership, thus creating an incongruity between the female gender role and the leadership role. The incongruence of female leadership creates two forms of prejudice for female leaders. The first form of prejudice is the incongruence between female leadership roles and gender roles whereas the second form of prejudice associated with female leaders demonstrating the organizational attributes associated with masculine leadership.

Social role theory. Social role theory refers to individuals behaving according to their gender, reinforced by gender stereotyping (Eagly & Karau, 2002; Eagly & Sczesny, 2009). Within the social role theory, "communal and agency attributes are the basis for the beliefs and ideas about women and men" (Eagly & Karau, 2002, p. 574). Communal characteristics based on the concern for the well-being or welfare of others, whereas organizational characteristics represented by aggressive and controlling behavior are noted (Eagly & Carli, 2007). Communal characteristics are associated with women, whereas organizational characteristics are associated with men.

Leadership has been associated with agency characteristics, in essence merging leadership with men. The perception of leadership as a male domain leaves female leaders facing a many barriers known as the labyrinth phenomenon (Eagly & Karau, 2002). Situations that require agency characteristics are not compatible with women as leaders; however, a meta-analysis of this investigation concluded men and women could both become leaders, on an equal basis within the social role perspective (Eagly & Karau, 2002).

Definitions of Terms

Gender role theory. The term gender role emerged in the 1970s in Europe and North American feminist movements. There are three interrelated aspects of the labyrinthine phenomenon function concurrently (Hoogland, 2007). First, gender is a feature of subjectivity conceived of and recognized in gendered terms, both individually, and collectively. Second, gender functions as a social variable, structuring the classification of people among peers. Secondary terms of sexual difference assume different social positions and pursue different and largely preordained life courses within a multi-stratified sociocultural realm. Third, gender designates the cultural representation and significations of the classifications for a man or a woman (Hoogland, 2007).

Glass ceiling. In 1991, the United States Department of Labor established the Glass Ceiling Commission that defined the glass ceiling as "those artificial barriers based on attitudinal or organizational bias that prevent qualified individuals from advancing upward in their organization into management-level positions"

(Hester, 2007, p. 1). The limitations imposed by such barriers according to Hester (2007) are typically various forms of discrimination often sexist. Hester further contends that these barriers are not at the peak of issues encountered by women executives alone, a labyrinth phenomenon is present and applicable only to women.

Labyrinth. The labyrinth phenomenon is metaphor symbolizing the complexities that hinder the paths (for women) to leadership (Eagly & Carli (2007). The labyrinth contains numerous ever-changing barriers, some subtle, unexpected, tortious, and otherwise blatantly obvious. Eagly and Carli (2007 and Eagly and Sczesny (2009) suggested the labyrinth is indicative of the numerous barriers and paths women encounter as they aspire leadership position in corporate offices. Women must navigate through the labyrinth, overcoming barriers, tortious twists, and abrupt dead ends to become leaders (Eagly & Carli, 2007; Eagly & Sczesny, 2009). The twisting and often tortious paths that women encounter trying to advance the corporate ladder are often derivative of organizational gender specific traditions.

Labyrinthine. Labyrinthine is indicative of the intricate series of winding paths in a form of complex mazes generated by traditions and practices related to divisional labor. The labyrinthine paths that women encounter hinder the advancement to executive leadership roles in corporate offices. Labyrinthine hindrances arise because of organizational traditions and practices that reflect the traditional family division of labor such as a mother's domestic responsibility to provide the lion's share of childcare (Eagly & Carli, 2007).

According to Eagly and Carli (2007), the labyrinthine phenomenon has a long history recognized throughout the world from ancient Greece to extending to contemporary leadership today. As a contemporary symbol, the labyrinthine phenomenon conveys the idea of a complex journey toward a striving goal e.g., the ascent to upper-level leadership. "Passage through a labyrinth is not simple or direct, but requires persistence, awareness of one's progress, and a careful analysis of the puzzles that lie ahead" (Eagly & Carli, 2007, p. 2). For women who aspire to obtain upper-level leadership roles, find their paths filled with irruptive twists and turns, both unexpected, and expected. Because all labyrinths have a viable route to the center, it also comprehended that goals are attainable, if one possess the stamina to endure the myriad of obstacles that occur.

Role conflict. Role conflict emerges when diverse expectations interrupt simultaneously, resulting in difference for the individual who attempts actively to combine dissimilar roles (Biddle & Thomas, 1979; Callero, 1994; Lynch, 2007; Rose, 1951; Turner, 1990). Dissimilar roles characteristically influenced by gender-based perceptions.

Sticky Floor. Theorizes that women do not advance because of self-inflected or self-imposed barriers based on belief of the inability to succeed; society isn't holding women back, but that women are holding themselves back (Shambaugh, 2007). According to Shambaugh (2007), the sticky floor phenomenon keeps women stuck to outmoded, self-defeating and, unconscious behaviors that impede advancement in the corporate arena. The sticky floor theory suggests that women undermine their organizational leadership advancement opportunities through self-sabotage (Shambaugh, 2007). Women do not pursue leadership opportunities because of low self-esteem and self-efficacy beliefs

Theory of male dominance. Theorizes that leadership is inherent to men; according to Brown (1999), men are naturally more dominant and competitive than women and therefore more likely to gain authoritative roles. Brown (1999) declared that differences in gender produce the same selective forces that cause behavioral gender differences; therefore leading to male competitiveness observed in the workplace. The basic premise, according to Brown (1999), is that leadership, and dominance more generally stems from traits built into the male through adaptation to primeval environments in which males evolve.

Assumptions

The assumptions of this investigation regard areas taken for granted by the research (McQueen et al., 2006; Neuman, 2007). Assumptions within the context of this investigation varied and ranged from participant responding with honesty and integrity, relationship and perceptions of coercion, associated with power and human relation, assumption of gender bias or opposing power structures, to emotional disruptions encountered.

The assumption of integrity and honesty of the participants of this investigation was evident in the responses provided each participant. The emotions that accompanied their responses also supported the assumption of integrity and honesty sufficiently met. Likewise, the assumption of relationships and coercion, associated with power and human relations the respondents provided example and experiences that corroborated the relationship assumption providing sufficient proof of this assumption.

Foundationally, the investivegative assumption of gender bias based on opposing power structures was met as the collection of data conveyed through participant responses. The emotional aspect of the assumptions of this investigation provided an inordinate amount of information and support to meet and exceed the assumptive posture of this investigation. The assumptions of participant's experiences provided a necessary and comprehensive perspective of the Labyrinth phenomenon through responses to the interview questions (McQueen et al. 2006). The assumptions of this investigative approach led to an exhaustive understanding of the labyrinth phenomenon.

Scope, Limitations, and Delimitations

Scope: The scope of this investigation was delimited to obtaining a comprehension of the phenomenon of the labyrinth theory as women aspire to achieve leadership roles in corporate America. The focus of this investigation is on women who, according to Eagly and Carli (2007), Eagly, and Sczesny (2009), navigates through the labyrinth of barriers, and dead-ends as they seek to obtain leadership roles in corporate America. The investigations provided a delimited nature of the examination of the opportunities or lack thereof for women in corporate arena.

Limitations: The sample size and limited geographical area of the investigation focused on two limitations of this investigation. The results are not generalizable to a larger population because of the small sample size and limited geographic boundaries (McQueen et al., 2006). However, the results contain comprehensive information on the experiences of the participants. Each participant participated in a 1-hour interview and discussion of each interview question. The results in this investigation are useful to the investigation of the labyrinth phenomenon experienced in the Pittsburgh corporate arena. Another limitation of this investigation was that the participants were entrepreneurial executive leaders within the constructs of private own businesses outside the standard business area of corporate America. This limitation resulted in assumptions, biases, and perceptions directly associated to these participants during the interviewing process. In addition, the investigation was limited to the small segment of responses.

Delimitations: The investigative process was delimited to the participants' direct knowledge and experiences of the labyrinth phenomenon. The investigative process was also delimited to exploring the experiences and perceptions of women in corporate leadership positions in Pittsburgh (McQueen et al., 2006). The research also included a review of glass ceiling theories and labyrinthine barriers. These barriers hinder the progress for women in their pursuit to corporate leadership (Eagly & Carli, 2007; Okafor & Amalu, 2010).

Summary

Chapter 1 included an overview of the of the labyrinth metaphor associated to the glass sticky floor (glass ceiling) theory within Pittsburgh, Pennsylvania corporate arena. The approach to this investigation presented a wealth of information, which enabled the development, and support of the labyrinth phenomenon. The initial perspective of this phenomenon began within the 1987 work of Dr. Eagly, a Northwestern University professor. Dr. Eagly's work began with a published work Sex Differences in Social Behavior: A Social-Role Interpretation. Twenty years later (2007), Dr Eagly along with Dr. Carli presented the provocative perspective of the labyrinth phenomenon in a study entitled: Through the Labyrinth: *The Truth About How Women Become Leaders*. This work became the foundation of this investigative work.

From this provocative work, other researcher examined the anomalies associated with gender bias, stereotypes, and women ascension to upper-level leadership roles. For example researchers such as Duehr and Bono, (2006), Hogue, (2010), Hoogland, (2007), Hopkins, O'Neil, and Bilimoria, (2006), presented studies focusing on various issues associated with women in business in relation to various hindrances that ranged from the glass ceiling and sticky floor to ethical conduct and stereotypical gender biases. The basis of these works developed a structural platform of exploration of the women in Pittsburgh, Pennsylvania's corporate offices. The expanse of research enabled this investigation to perform an exhaustive exploration of women in corporate leadership roles.

The research included the strategic problems and the deficiency of advancement among women in corporate offices, Pittsburgh, Pennsylvania. Using an IPA phenomenological research approach provided insight into the experiences of women in Pittsburgh, Pennsylvania. This phenomenological research resulted in a greater understanding of the hindrances imposed by labyrinthine phenomenon relevant to issues women encounter the Pittsburgh corporate arena. Chapter 2 includes a comprehensive examination of literature, studies, and relevant findings.

Chapter 2: Literature Review

This research was a fact-finding investigation of executive leadership in the Pittsburgh corporate arena. The literature review of the barriers associated to the scope of this research is not a comprehensive examination of the barrier, but rather an examination of the labyrinthine phenomenon associated to the lack of advancement for women in leadership positions in corporate offices Pittsburgh, Pennsylvania.

The phenomenon of the sticky floor as a result of the well-known glass ceiling is often associated to the difficulties women encounter as they pursue executive endeavors. The association between the sticky floor and the labyrinth phenomenon vary immensely. The hindrances women encounter known as sticky floor phenomenon according to Shambaugh (2007) is a directly associated to the failure of women to recognize abilities and or refusal to pursue because they do not believe in their ability to succeed. Whereas according to Eagly, et al., (2007) hindrances and obstacles women encounter as result of the labyrinth phenomenon are directly associated to women who departed or strayed off course from their executive pursuits to handle life events (family obligations, education, or health issues).

As women seek to return to their prior executive goals, an assumptive perception of inability to perform is imposed (Haney, 2010). Immediately, women encounter deliberate acts of sabotage, torturous twist and unrealistic demand or constraints applied to the position (Eagly, et. al., 2007). The extent of demand and pressure has prompted women to reconsider their pursuits in executive leadership. This investigation discovered a number of women (93 percent), who have either accepted the imposed constraints, (five percent), decided to exit the corporate arena and pursue business or entrepreneurial endeavors or women (two percent) continue to engage the imposed constraints and fight for upper-level leadership roles (Eagly et al, 2007).

In the exploration of the labyrinthine phenomenon, the sticky floor (as well as the glass ceiling) is a misnomer continually suggested as a rationale for the lack of female presence in executive offices. In direct contrast to tortures of unyielding twists and turns of the labyrinthine phenomenon imposed on women who return to the corporate arena. The sticky floor also suggests the lack of women's presence in upper-level leadership roles is a direct result of the low self-esteem, and lack of confidence or belief in the ability to perform at an executive level (Shambaugh, 2007).

The investigation of the labyrinth phenomenon expressly addressed the aftermath experiences women encounter after fulfilling life events obligations. Focusing on the enormity and effects of these torturous twists and turns imposed on women attempting to return to male-dominated corporate arenas presents a vivid and holistic perspective of the challenges women encounter in Pittsburgh, Pennsylvania's corporate arena.

Chapter 2 includes several sections that provide the foundation for this investigative approach with emphasis on the labyrinthine phenomenon for women in executive leadership roles the Pittsburgh corporate offices. The sections include a literature review that involves research of approximately 230 peer-reviewed articles, books, government documents, and Internet websites. The second section includes literature to address the topics of (a) gender and business history (b) the glass ceiling theory and barriers (c) the labyrinth theory and barriers, and (c) corporate America and the workplace. The literature review includes theories and findings relevant to the research questions of this investigation and includes a discussion of the labyrinthine phenomenon associated to women in corporate America.

Historical Overview

The social attitude toward women in executive leadership positions is very dissimilar from attitudes toward men in executive leadership positions (Musteen, Baker, & Baeten, 2006). Though women have made progress in the workplace, they still encounter barriers that affect aspirations of leadership. Throughout the history of women in the workplace, the value, and contribution of women are not recognize by a society that historically has accepted and celebrated by men (Catalyst, 2012; Eagly & Carli, 2007; Koenig, Eagly, Mitchell, & Ristikari, 2011).

History of Women and Gender Roles in the Workplace

From the 18th century to the present day, women have pursued entrepreneurial endeavors beyond the socio-cultural views on women roles (Hebert & Link, 2006). Stereotypically, the view of the role of working women was as stay-at-home household managers, rearing children as the support of the family. Hebert and Link (2006) declared in the United States during the late eighteenth century the domination of women began with the development of services as part of the U.S. national economy.

Women began work as domestic workers, provided personal services, such as nursing, millinery dressmaking, and hairdressing; and by the nineteenth century, advanced into clerical and retailing work (Kwolek-Folland, 2007). As women ventured beyond the home to start their professions, businesses were small, labor-intensive, slow growing, and service-oriented retailing operations. Typically, women entrepreneurs were considered divorced, widowed, or at home with small children, and starting businesses out of financial necessity (Davis, Capobianco, & Kraus, 2010).

Between 1950 and 1990, the largest proportions of service workers in every sector of business in the United States were women (Kessler-Harris, 2004; Kwolek-Folland, 2007). Although numerous laws were established outlawing discrimination on the basis of gender in the U.S. segregation continued during the 1960s and 1970s (Kwolek-Folland, 2001). Women entering new fields such as managers, proprietors, and workers, skill content, and social statuses downgraded, and perceived these fields as suitable for women. Suggesting the perception of women professionals populating these environments, past, and present are shaped by the ideas of domestic labor and services (Davis et al., 2010; Kessler-Harris, 2004; Kwolek-Folland, 2001, 2007; Koenig, Eagly, Mitchell, & Ristikari, 2011).

Glass Ceiling Theory

With the establishment of the Glass Ceiling Commission by the U.S. Department of Labor in 1991, the glass ceiling was defined as an artificial barrier based upon attitudes and organizational biases preventing advancement of women into executive level positions (Hester, 2007). Hester (2007) argued the limitations imposed by such barriers typically based on various forms of discrimination often gender-related affect women in corporate America. The theory of a persisting glass ceiling theory is one of the most controversial and sensitive aspects of employment equality in corporate America (Grout, Park, & Sonderegger, 2007).

Eagly and Carli (2007), Güngör and Biernat (2009), and Hogue (2010), challenged leaders to revisit the interpretations of the glass ceiling metaphor and examine the complexities of labyrinthine obstacles women encounter in their pursuit of executive leadership in corporate America. Hogue (2010) challenged the ideas that equality has been achieved in the workplace; emphatically arguing that the complexities and labyrinthine obstacles of work life experiences women encounter persist and remain multifaceted (Hogue, 2010). Eagly and Carli and Hogue recommended to leadership in corporate America to revisit the current thinking and address the labyrinth phenomenon. Suggesting than an in-depth analysis of the various barriers women currently encounter is beneficial to creating a cohesive and diverse workplace.

Current Barriers

Barreto, Ryan, and Schmitt (2009) proposed that continuing gender discrimination, role incongruity, sexism, and wage gap barriers toward women continue to be obstacles within every corporate arena and therefore, making the extent of women's advancement an uncertainty. Explanations on social commentary and opinion offer numerous, conflicting reports of women advancing in the corporate arena is founded on the likelihood that gender discrimination is a genuine problem for women today (Barreto, Ryan, & Schmitt, 2009). Reports (Catalyst 2008, 2011; Organization for Economic Cooperation and Development, 2008) indicate the perspective that women have progressively made clear advances, moving into previously male-dominated positions. Reports continue to show women remain underrepresented in positions of power in corporate offices throughout America.

An additional aspect of barriers women encounter in corporate offices, according to Heilman and Eagly (2008), are role incongruity. Role incongruity occurs when women leadership is devalued. This perceived notion implies that women are less promising for leadership roles than males. Heilman and Eagly declared this perspective of negative performance expectations, produces biased evaluations is a continuing barrier of discrimination for women in corporate America (Heilman & Eagly, 2008).

Barriers to Women's Advancement

According to Eagly and Carli (2008) based on images of the labyrinth phenomenon barriers in upper level management in corporate America are far more significant than originally perceived. Continuing, Eagly and Carli declared the suppositions surrounding the inordinate appeal of the glass ceiling metaphor are misleading. Eagly and Carli further emphasized that the existence of women in upper level management refutes the premise of a glass ceiling metaphor. However, the reality of the glass metaphor is that women do not encounter discrimination late in their professional pursuits but from the beginning of their career aspirations in corporate arenas. These discriminatory occurrences and interruptions refer to navigating a labyrinth (Eagly & Carli, 2008; Heilman & Eagly, 2008).

Labyrinth

The labyrinth phenomenon presents continual intricate twisting and winding hurdles that are unexpected or unwarranted often transparent challenges that are unexpected. According to Eagly and Carli, (2007); Heilman and Eagly, (2008), women encounter a labyrinthine phenomenon while seeking leadership roles. Encountering challenges that are frequently changing, complex, and numerous. The difficulties women encounter stem from obstacles associated to balancing career and family (Eagly &Carli, 2007; Heilman & Eagly, 2008).

Conversely, the premise of the labyrinth metaphor acknowledges obstacles but is not ultimately discouraging. "If women understand the various barriers that make up the labyrinth, and how some women find their way around them, then women may work more effectively to improve the situation" (Eagly & Carli, 2007, p. 2). These discriminatory effects of the labyrinth anomalies women's encounter hinders advancement is present in corporate offices throughout America (Eagly & Carli, 2008).

Labyrinthine

The labyrinthine metaphor (Eagly & Carli, 2007, 2008) shows the depth of twisting obstacles women in Pittsburgh, Pennsylvania's corporate offices encounter. For example, the labyrinthine obstacles of family responsibilities for women often end leadership pursuits. Eagly and Carli (2007, 2008) posited that women take on family responsibilities at a far greater extent than men take and often leave their jobs for family reasons. As a result, women who leave their jobs to handle the responsibilities of child rearing particularly at the prime of a woman's career face major setbacks. Consequently, many women fail to return to a good career trajectory or prior level of pay or authority, and upon returning to work often settle for less challenging part time positions (Eagly & Carli, 2008; Eagly & Sczesny, 2009). Setbacks such as this often result in advancement, reduction in pay, demotions, and responsibilities often resulting in women abandoning their pursuits to upper-level leadership (Heilman & Eagly, 2008).

Gender Differences

The widely debated issue of gender difference remains an important subject in business development (Eagly, 1987). Gender differences, as defined by Al-Lamky and Aysa (2007), are the behavior and classification, culture or psychological traits typically associated to a particular sex. Possessing different attitudes, behaviors, physical, and biological attributes, and reactions that separate characteristically and distinctively perceived (Biagi, 2005). Within the workplace, these gender differences play a major and often unfair role in the determination of skills and qualifications of women in corporate America.

Gender Role Theory

The term gender emerged in the 1970s in Europe and North American feminist movements. European and North American feminism served to liberate women from the marginalized oppression in a male-dominated society and to expose the male-bias subterfuge that kept women in a subordinate role based on their reproductive capacities (Eagly, 1987).

Three aspects are function concurrently and in interrelated behaviors within the expanding domain of gender theory (Hoogland, 2007). First, gender is a feature of subjectivity conceived of and recognized in gendered terms, both individually, and collectively. Second, gender functions as a social variable, structuring the ways in which people are classified. These secondary terms of sexual difference are inclined to assume social positions, pursue diverse, and largely preordained life courses within a multiply stratified sociocultural realm. Third, gender designates the cultural representations and significations of what it are classifies as a man or woman (Hoogland, 2007).

Theory of Male Dominance

The theory of male dominance stems from a socio-cultural perspective that proposes over time males have evolved differently from females (Distelhorst, 2005). Gender differences between men and women, according to Seidman (2004), are social, hierarchical differences between men and women produces reasons for male dominance. Seidman further proposed the gender order is hierarchical and men are consistently in a position of dominance.

Advocating beliefs that women and men experiences are different in every issue of dominance and deference (Distelhorst, 2005; Seidman, 2004). The perspective Distelhorst (2005) declared the association between gender behaviors and dominance begins at birth and reinforced by societal interactions with and from family, peers, and school interactions. The characteristics of male dominance in other words become a curriculum taught by societal beliefs established by assumptions, beliefs, and values about how women and men should interact and conduct themselves. For example in competitive situations, males go all-out to win; in hierarchical situations, males take charge and in situations of individuality males stand-on-your- own. Behaviors such as these are considered appropriate and dominant behavior for men. Whereas, women are to socialize, liaise, and cooperate in situations with a focus on child rearing, family, and homemaking. Therefore, men dominate, and control from birth (Distelhorst, 2005; Seidman, 2004).

Social barriers are barriers to access created by the socio-cultural way of thinking, specifically, the behaviors toward other people or things. These barriers are supposed as behavioral norms that encompass the hostile environment and treatment (blatant discrimination in the workplace, promotional denial, salary reduction, and sexual harassment), and unrealistic demands toward others (Welle & Heilman, 2005). Welle, and Heilman (2005) suggested social barriers and acts of social exclusion subtle or overtly performed are equivalent to discrimination barriers to women that impede advancement in corporate America.

These social barriers and socio-cultural practices create conflict in the roles of leadership for women. Role conflict (Lynch, 2007) occurs when diverse expectations interrupt simultaneously, resulting in difference for the individual who attempts actively to combine dissimilar roles (Biddle & Thomas, 1979; Callero, 1994; Lynch, 2007; Rose, 1951; Turner, 1990).

Stereotypes

According to Eagly and Sczesny (2009), cultural stereotypes for women in corporate America often reflected as lacking the ability to perform important leadership roles. These perceptions add to the barriers encountered by women pursuing roles with important power and authority. Eagly and Sczesny's research on cultural masculinity stereotypes and leadership contained paradigms characteristic of cultural beliefs of masculinity dominating femininity in organizations. Positing organizations within a masculine cultural environment think males are better suited in decision-making leadership positions. Whereas, women are less desirable in leadership roles because of compassion and empathy that interferes with corporate decision making (Eagly & Sczesny, 2009).

Organizational Barriers

Organizational barriers are as factors that prevent organizations from implementing, and factors that reduce the effectiveness of family-supportive benefits and policies after they are in place (Eagly, 1987). Researchers (Briggs, Jaramillo, & Weeks, 2011; Eagly, & Carli 2007; Eagly & Karua, 2002; Eagly & Sczesny, 2009; Savage-Austin & Honeycutt 2011; Van den Steen, 2010) identified organizational barriers as gender role assumptions, lack of national policy, rigid schedules, lack of management support, and corporate culture. These barriers work in conjunction preventing organizations from successfully developing family supported environments (Van den Steen, 2010).

Another perspective associated to organizational barriers presented in a 2011 research conducted by Savage-Austin and Honeycutt (2011). In this research, Savage-Austin and Honeycutt discussed organizational barriers as they relate to servant leadership theory. Postulating the philosophy of servant leadership addressed the different way of understanding the responsibility of leadership, which acts as a steward over his or her area of responsibility. Organizational leaders assume the attitude, roles, and services of leaders and followers in his or her socio-cultural environment. In this sense, Van den Steen declared organizational barriers operating under the theory of servant leadership unintentionally operate in a sense of shared values and beliefs that influence culture and performance negatively for women in corporate America (Van den Steen, 2010).

Professional Development

The workplace has changed and made advances for women in the workplace there remain several basic ideologies in corporate America hindering professional advancement and equality for women (Haney, 2010). There are a number of ideologies-related professional development and difficulties women encounter. The most significant ideologies are organizations who maintain a glass ceiling method of operations, sexual harassment, and sexism in the workplace, socio-cultural gender biases that begin at childhood, Labyrinthine phenomenon, and lack of support for educational pursuits, child rearing, and family obligations, and competition. Additionally included in a list of ideologies are divisiveness between women caused by fewer positions available in the workplace (Berry & Franks, 2010; Davis et al., 2010; Distelhorst, 2005; Eagly & Carli, 2007; Eagly & Sczesny, 2009; Güngör & Biernat 2009; Haney, 2010; Pârlea-Buzatu, 2011; Saruman, 2011).

Development

Leadership development is crucial to women professionals seeking advancement in corporate America. Ely, Ibarra, and Kolb

(2011) suggested educational developments and timely approaches in organizations indicate efforts to create leadership development programs for women seeking to executive leadership roles. Recent efforts, however; have failed in areas of leadership and education perpetuating ineffective framework and lack of comprehensible, theoretical, and implementable leadership programs for women (Eagly et al., 2007; Ely et al., 2011; Hewlett, 2007; Zahidi & Ibarra, 2010).

Lacking the necessary developmental framework many organizations have resorted to placing women in token leadership positions; an approach Martin and Meyerson (1998) coined as "add-women-and-stir" (p. 312). Organizations that function under this assumption that gender should not matter in the development of leadership training, extend to women the identical education and training as men (Ely et al., 2011; Hewlett, 2007; Zahidi & Ibarra, 2010).

Women in Corporate America

Zahidi and Ibarra (2010) declared the most important factor of an organizational competitiveness is education, human talent/skills, and productivity within the workforce. In corporate America, women account for greater than half of college and university graduates, resulting in dramatic changes in gender gaps in higher education. Thus, women are creating greater percentage of talent available to corporate America (Zahidi & Ibarra, 2010). In time, Ely et al. (2010) proclaimed that corporate America's competitive effectiveness will significantly depend on if and how it uses its female talent. To date, women in corporate America in Fortune 500 leadership positions have stagnant in recent years (Catalyst, 2011).

Demographics

The 2010 Catalyst census report for the United States labor force indicated women made up 46.7% of the labor force, 58.6% of working women had 16 years or more of service in the labor force, compared to 71.2% of males in the labor force. Women composed 51.5% of management, professional, or related positions. Minority women (African American) composed 5.2% (2,751,000) of all people employed in management and related positions. Whereas, Asian American women composed 2.8%, and Latinas comprised 3.8% of all people employed in management, professional, or related positions. The participation of parents with children under the age of 18 in the labor force represented 70.8%, and 93.7% for fathers, and 56.5% of all mothers with children under the age (Catalyst, 2010).

Labyrinth Phenomenon and Corporate America

Eagly and Carli (2007) discussed labyrinthine phenomenon resulting from socio-cultural barriers and the consequences of prejudice and discrimination observed and interpreted socially. Gender stereotypes associated to prescribed gender cues associated with organizational leadership predominantly evokes a masculine association to upper-level leadership roles. Such associations leave women vulnerable to prejudices that define women as incapable of performing at upper-level leadership roles (Eagly & Sczesny, 2009).

Gender biases often consider women as unqualified and lacking stereotypical male attributes of leadership. Women encounter criticism if they display male attributes of leadership whereas other women encounter rejection because they embrace feminine traits. Organizational stereotypes and beliefs often become deeply entrenched and difficult to change (Davis et al., 2010; Eagly & Carli, 2007; Eagly & Sczesny, 2009).

Factors Influencing Women's Representation in Corporate America

Fiedler (1967) suggested leadership behavior was an act or behavior of an individual involved in coordinating, directing, and influencing groups of individuals. Socio-cultural behavior equated to leadership power that forms and influence relationships in the workplace, these influences may be blatant or ambiguous (Bass, 1990). House, Hanges, Javidan, Dorfman, and Gupta (2004) studied the importance of gender and gender ratio, individual characteristics, and societal cultural perceptions in leadership behaviors that influence women representation in corporate America.

Leadership behaviors influencing women in corporate America are characteristic of differences such as competencies, motives, personality traits, and perceived socio-cultural skills (Yukl

& Lepsinger, 2005). Leadership influences also depend on organizational culture embedded in societal cultures that influence leadership behaviors and influence the progress of women seeking executive leadership roles in corporate America (Davis et al., 2010). A societal cultural trait associated to gender developed early in childhood, founded on family belief and dynamics, and in the communities and schools. Organizational practices cultured through socialization at the workplace (Davis et al., 2010).

Women Advancing in Corporate America

The challenges women encounter continues to pose problems for advancement to executive level leadership positions in corporate America that women cannot dismantle alone. Employment discrimination, gender bias organizational policies, and biases in domestic responsibilities contribute to and impede the advancement of women in corporate America (Eagly & Carli, 2007). Women seeking to move beyond these obstacles will have to become adaptable to their socio-cultural workplace environment (Greenwald, 2006).

Moving toward equality, Eagly and Carli (2007) declared requires the ability to adapt to a male-dominated environment. Adaptability requires women to combine outstanding proficiency with warmth and approachability, be assertive, recognize self-worth, become proficient negotiators, to build communal confidence on-the-job, and pursue peer-to-peer mentoring (Eagly & Carli, 2007; Greenwald, 2006; Henry-Brown & Campbell-Lewis, 2005; Hinton, 2006). The supposition is, as women continue to make cultural changes in, abilities, education, career ambitions, job preferences, personalities, and workplace participation increases, organizations, and culture may change (Eagly & Carli, 2007; Hopkins, O'Neil & Bilimoria, 2006).

Summary

A number of leadership traits detailed the ideas of diversity and the inclusion of women in executive leadership roles. For this research investigation, there were four areas of concern about leadership opportunities for women are (a) labyrinth phenomenon, (b) socio-cultural stereotypes, and (c) organizational culture (Eagly

& Carli, 2007; Greenwald, 2006). Studies indicated the socio-cultural gender relations, and leadership behaviors, internally, and externally within organizational structures in corporate America (Eagly & Carli, 2007; Greenwald, 2006; Henry-Brown & Campbell-Lewis, 2005; Hinton, 2006; Hopkins, O'Neil & Bilimoria, 2006).

The organizational leadership can influence workplace interaction and progress of women to executive leadership positions. Theorists suggested that socio-cultural and socio-economic differences negatively affect organizational environments. Organizational structures are composed of male-dominated workforce, presenting a continuing lack of diversity, rewarding competition based on gender, and societal differences influence corporate leadership. Though women possess the knowledge and leadership skills to ascend the corporate ladder to the executive suite women remain underrepresented in executive leadership roles in most organizations in corporate America (Catalyst, 2010; 2011; U.S. Department of labor, 2009). Chapter 3 includes research method, design, population, sampling, and data collection, validity, and analysis.

Chapter 3: Methodology

The labyrinthine phenomenon women encounter in pursuit to executive level in corporate America was the focus of this qualitative, phenomenological investigation. Exploration indicates the perceptions of the labyrinth phenomenon and the connection of the underrepresentation of women in executive leadership in corporate America (Eagly et al., 2007 & 2009). The results of this investigation added to the leadership literature and identify some perceptions that hinder women's advancement to executive leadership roles. Chapter 3 includes a comprehensive discussion of the research methodology and includes the following sections: (a) research method; (b) design appropriateness; (c) population, sampling, and data collection; (d) validity and reliability; and (e) data analysis.

Research Method

The investigative approach focused on a qualitative method, which was appropriate for examining the perceptions of possible reasons for the underrepresentation of women in corporate America using interviews with current women in corporate America. This investigative process involved using open-ended interview questions and analyzing the data to identify themes in the participants' responses. Using the qualitative method enabled the exploration of meaning through an overlapping recursive process (Leedy & Ormrod, 2010).

The qualitative method is used to explore broad views of data making assessments across social situations supported by five main goals (McQueen et al., 2006; Neuman, 2005). According to Neuman (2005), these goals are construct a theory founded on the premise and not test a theory. Acquire a mechanism of collecting data, e.g., comprehensive interviewing, and questions. Reflect the probability the phenomenological research has alternative meanings for the investigation. Acquire a systematic method to address the phenomenon, and acquiring the proper tool for data analysis to categorize and form the developing theme of the phenomenon (Leedy & Ormrod, 2010; McQueen et al., 2006; Neuman, 2005).

Research Design

The phenomenological design used in the investigation sought to collect supportive data via face-to-face interviewing that associated with the awareness of the labyrinthine negativity or increased negatively experienced in the pursuit of executive leadership. According to information reported in research conducted by Eagly and Carli (2007), the issues attached to the difficulties women encounter in their pursuits to upper executive offices extend beyond the known glass ceiling metaphor grounded on the labyrinthine effects encountered as women reenter the workforce. The intent of the investigation was to explore the labyrinth theory to validate or refute the labyrinthine theory women encounter in the workplace. The potential risks and stressors of this investigative process were the participant might have been made aware of difficulties and negative treatment they were not aware of previously. This new awareness might have heightened negative reactions or interactions ranging from the position currently held to imposing ranking authority.

Participants might also have felt resentment with the introduction of the new information. The process of identifying and quantifying risks involved mitigating the risks to the participant (Sapolsky, 2004). The following strategies helped mitigate potential risks and stressors for the interview participant. First, confidence and comprehension of the subject matter were conveyed. The researcher was knowledgeable and nonbiased when beginning the interview process. An atmosphere was established to facilitate in the participant a sense of confidence and comfort entering into the discussion of the topic.

Second, the researcher was observant, aware of the participant's body language facial expressions, changes in posture, tone of voice, and signs of irritation (e.g., agitation, annoyance, aggravation). Non-visual cues, such as a sense of discomfort or uneasiness not physically visible by sensed in the response(s) given. Third, also considered were the cognitive of responses to the subject matter. The flow of information was monitored in both timing and quantity as a way of limiting the amount of stress, knowledge (new or otherwise) about the actuality of their environmental situation may produce (or is producing) in the workplace.

Fourth, confidence was extended to balance with any overwhelming, uneasiness in the participant. The participant was reassured that the information she provided was confidential and the participants would remain anonymous. Fifth, a systematic approach was taken, expounding on the participant's capacity for self-efficacy to control the future. The participant was encouraged to discuss her known strengths, achievements, and attributes that have made her successful. Sixth, a method for ending the interview was prepared in case the interview appeared to become too stressful for the participant. The method involved expressing much gratitude for participation in the investigative approach.

Interpretive phenomenological analysis (IPA) framework structure for analyzing qualitative research data collected for women in Pittsburgh Pennsylvania's corporate research provided a perspective of the information collected. The first major approach to qualitative research is phenomenology (e.g., descriptive studies of individuals experiences associated with a phenomenon). Therefore, an investigation exploring the meaning, structure, and essence of the lived experiences of a phenomenon by an individual or by many individuals provides access to individuals' life-worlds, which is their world of experience; it is where consciousness exists.

Phenomenological researchers often search for commonalities across individuals (rather than only focusing on what is unique to a single individual). For example, what are the essences of peoples' experience of an individual who has to take a leave from work to deal family responsibilities or, what are the essences of peoples' experiences of an uncaring corporate official when sudden life event or circumstances occur an IPA method was appropriate and provided information necessary for analysis.

Within the IPA phenomenological research, process case studies provide detailed interpretations and analysis of one or more aspect of investigation. The foundational aspect of case studies questions the characteristics of a premise or comparison of premises. In this case, the foundational aspect of this investigation examined women within the corporate arena in Pittsburgh, Pennsylvania inclusive of every person, group, activity (positive or negative), and process in which these actions occur. A phenomenological investigation, incorporating a case study approach is applicable.

Providing multiple methods of data collection e.g., interviews, observation, documents, and questionnaires providing vivid and detailed description of the lived experiences.

The phenomenological design were appropriate for this investigation using face-to-face interviews to obtain participant data on corporate America. The approach was a suitable process for collecting the experiences of women's work experiences to review the perceptions on the labyrinth phenomenon that imped their ascent to executive leadership. Using the quantitative method would not have been an effective approach to this investigation because of the subjects of this investigative premise.

In this investigation, the process of data collection consisted of face-to-face, interview, digital audio tapping. Each scheduled interview was conducted off-sight or in a neutral environment of the participant's choice. The investigation did not require or involve the observation of participants in their work environment. The information obtained through this investigation did not require data compilation or manipulation. The goal of this investigation is to explain the association of one variable with another, typically using several cases (Krueger & Neuman, 2006). With the comprehension, that conducting a qualitative investigation provides the opportunity to examine patterns of similarities and differences across cases and to try to some to terms with their diversity (McQueen & Zimmerman, 2006; Shank, 2006).

Conducting a phenomenological analysis for this investigation resulted in gaining comprehension of the labyrinthine paths women have encountered in pursuit of executive leadership positions. McQueen et al. (2006) and Shank (2006) suggested that a phenomenological process should begin with the individual's awareness of the world, which was appropriate for this investigative approach that led to the insightful meaning of the similarities and differences of the participants' perceived environment (McQueen et al., 2006; Shank, 2006). The participants consisted of women in Pittsburgh corporate offices. There are several of the nation's major corporations in Pittsburgh, including the following: Pittsburgh Plate Glass Industries, Pittsburgh National Corporations, Mellon Bank Corporation, Mylan Incorporated, H J Heinz Company, FreeMarkets, Calgon Carbon Corporation, Bayer Corporation,

American Eagle Outfitters, Allegheny Technologies, 84 Lumber, US Airways, and Westinghouse.

Research Questions

- R1. What barriers do women in Pittsburgh, Pennsylvania's corporate office perceive as inhibiting their promotion in the workplace?
- R2. What are the reasons women are leaving Pittsburgh, Pennsylvania's corporate offices, and abandoning the pursuit of executive leadership roles?

The phenomenological design of this investigation was appropriate for using face-to-face interviews to obtain participant data on Pittsburgh corporate offices. The method investigation also provided approaches suitable for collecting data on the involvements of women's work experiences to review the perceptions on the labyrinth phenomenon that impede their ascent to executive leadership. The requirement for participation: 1) women between the ages 40-55 who have experienced life events that influenced or affected their pursuit to upper-level leadership, 2) Women who have held or currently hold leadership positions in Pittsburgh, Pennsylvania's corporate arena; and 3) women who separated from the corporate arena to pursue entrepreneurial endeavors.

The process of data collection consisted of face-to-face interviews, which were digitally (audio) recorded. Each designated interview was conducted at an off-sight area in a neutral environment of the participant's choice. This investigative process did not involve observing participants in their work environments. The data that desired for this investigation did not require manipulation. In a quantitative research, the goal is to explain the association of one variable with another, typically using several cases. Using the qualitative method may have been appropriate for examining patterns of similarities and differences across cases and coming to terms with their diversity (McQueen et al., 2006; Shank, 2006).

Population, Sample, and Sampling Method

This investigative intent was to explore the labyrinth phenomenon and the relationship to women in executive leadership roles in Pittsburgh. A review of the population, sampling, and data collection is primary to this approach. The purpose of this investigation was to develop comprehension of the labyrinth experiences women encounter previously associated with the glass ceiling theory. Eagly and Carli (2007) proposed instead of the unyielding glass ceiling, a labyrinth is an unrestricted and open-ended maze of events that hamper the progress of some women. Eagly and Carli further suggested some women manage to navigate successfully the ever-changing labyrinthine phenomenon and achieve their goals for success.

A labyrinth begins to form as women strategically maneuver between continuing discrimination, family responsibilities, and stereotypical bigotry. Eagly and Carli (2007) contended some women successfully maneuver these obstacles and find their way through the labyrinth and reach executive offices. The labyrinth phenomenon hampers many women to the degree of separation from corporate offices ending their pursuit of upper-level leadership. The goal of the investigative approach was to provide comprehension of the working conditions within Pittsburgh's corporate arena and explain the conditions presented by the labyrinthine theory that has become the new hindrance associated with women in corporate offices. Sampling included members of Pittsburgh, Pennsylvania's corporate offices and only those personnel who met the criteria (McQueen et al., 2006; Neuman, 2006). The participants were women in executive management position in Pittsburgh corporate offices.

The participant recruitment process began with an exploration of various Fortune 500 (or higher) businesses located in Pittsburgh, Pennsylvania. Additionally, and exploration of every Pittsburgh business corporate publication associated with or in discussion of the corporate offices located in Pittsburgh. Incorporated in the exploration of corporate and entrepreneurial businesses a thorough examination of women owned companies in Pittsburgh, Pennsylvania produced an eclectic and extensive participant pool for further examination to meet the studies requirements.

For example, this thorough examination included publications such as the Pittsburgh Businesstimes, Book of lists,

Business Women First, PGH Business News, Made in PA, Pitt*Business*, and Pittsburgh Technology Council, provided access to an extensive list of public and private companies owned and operated by women in Pittsburgh, Pennsylvania. Further examination of these and other publications presented a list of the top ranking companies, entrepreneurial endeavor of each company, level of business networking and competitive landscape of company operations.

Correspondingly, within these publications, readers have access to active forums that speak to or address issues women have or are currently encountering. Providing, an extensive pool of information of women in various stages of their professional careers. These stages represent women actively in leadership roles, women who have stepped down to pursue life events such as educational advancements, family responsibilities inclusive of but not limited to maternity leave, child, and parental care, to health issues. Accessing this information provided an opportunity to enlist prospective participants for this investigation. Results of this approach provided eleven of the participants examined. A simple plea to various forums and offices inquiring an interest in participating in research related to life events presented the remaining five perspective participants. These sources also provided additional information on women executive roles to obtain potential participants currently within Pittsburgh corporate region.

Based upon a review of the publication material previously listed, several major Fortune 500 corporations were identified as having corporate offices in Pittsburgh. These Fortune 500 corporations include Pittsburgh Plate Glass Industries, Pittsburgh National Corporations, Mellon Bank Corporation, Mylan Incorporated, H J Heinz Company, FreeMarkets, Calgon Carbon Corporation, Bayer Corporation, American Eagle Outfitters, Allegheny Technologies, 84 Lumber, US Airways, and Westinghouse. The executives who met the participant criteria for this investigative approach received an invitation to participate. Participation in this investigation was solely the decision of the participant. The individuals who agreed to participate were current or former executive officers and directors; in pursuit of upper executive positions in Pittsburgh's corporate arena or who had separated from the corporate arena to pursue, entrepreneurial endeavors in Pittsburgh, Pennsylvania as a result of the labyrinthine phenomenon experiences. Upon agreement to participate in this investigative process, interviews of the identified women executives in Pittsburgh began.

Informed Consent and Confidentiality

Participants were required to sign an informed consent form prior to the interviews. An introduction and defined confidentiality agreement were included in the introduction letter. The informed consent document indicated the participant's right to refuse to participate, withdraw from, and decline any aspect of investigation during the interview.

The anonymity and confidentiality procedures of the participants began the moment they consented to participate. Each participant was designated an ID tag that was associated with all data collected from the participant during the investigation. To ensure confidentiality of all interviewees no interview was conducted in personal business offices or on corporate property. All data collected was for the sole purpose of this investigation. No participants' or participants' companies' names were used during this investigation. All investigation materials will be stored in a locked location for 3 years following the investigation, after which all collected materials will during this investigation will be destroy by deletion of and or shredding of all data.

Instrumentation

The instrument used to acquire data from the participants consisted of face-to-face interviews using open-ended questions. The use of digital recording (audiotaping) during the face-to-face interview (with the consent of the participant) helped ensure exact information was collected specific to the premise of the labyrinth theory.

The interview questions developed as a result of research on the Labyrinth phenomenon. The content of literature review (Eagly et al., 2007 & 2008; Cohen, 2011; & Cox, 2012), and comparison of the region in question, Pittsburgh, Pennsylvania's corporate arena, further guided the development of the interview questions. As the questions developed, a pilot study to assured validity was conducted.

From the review and feedback of the pilot study the questions connected to this investigation developed. Participants specifically discussed her interpretation of the questions in association to the labyrinthine phenomenon. The discussion addressed redundancy, necessity, and relevance to the nature of the investigative approach. Questions one, three, and seven were modified and two questions were eliminated resulting in the final 16-participant questionnaire.

The design of the questions produced dialog and provided the participant with an opportunity to express information on how life events may have affected her pursuits of executive leadership positions in Pittsburgh. The interview questions resulted in an exhaustive discussion of the experiences in Pittsburgh corporate offices. The participants in the investigation had opportunities to clarify and expound vague or abbreviated comments.

Data Collection

The method of data collection for the investigation was a semi-structured face-to-face interviewing. The participants were contacted by phone to establish meeting times and locations. Conducting scheduled interviews at the designated time and using established questions prompted discussion on women in leadership and their workplace environment (McQueen et al., 2006; Leedy & Ormrod, 2010; Shank, 2006). The interviewing process in this investigation involved open-ended questioning that allowed for a greater comprehension of women leadership and their workplace environments. The goal of this investigation was to elicit dialog and narratives to develop a comprehensive analysis of the topic.

Credibility and Dependability

The members selected from various levels of leadership and disciplines investigation in Pittsburgh corporate office strengthen the credibility and dependability of the current. Reliability was established through the pursuit of this investigation, as analysis of the participants' responses resulted in themes and similarities encountered in various levels of leadership and disciplines in corporate America (McQueen et al., 2006; Neuman, 2007; Shank, 2006).

Internal validity. Validity includes internal, external, and statistical validity. Internal validity is indicative of no internal design errors whereas external validity provides the ability to generalize results in qualitative research. Statistical validity is representative of choosing the correct statistical procedure and meeting all assumptions for the investigation (McQueen et al., 2006; Neuman, 2007).

In the investigation, the participants were allowed to share perceptions of their workplace environment. The approach and process of this investigation helped ensure the accuracy of the information obtained and validated that the information is accurate. The process of validating the actuality of collected information required concise analysis of the collected data. Examining the data provided validation of the premise of this investigation.

External validity. External validity regards the ability to transfer assumptions or data of an inviestagion to other frameworks and situations (McQueen et al., 2006; Neuman, 2007; Leedy & Ormrod, 2010). This qualitative investigation explored the labyrinth theory and phenomenon, focusing on women executive leadership roles in corporations within Pittsburgh, Pennsylvania. The purpose of the investigation was to identify similarities and themes encountered within the sample of women, 40-55, in upper level leadership roles or who were pursuing upper level roles or had abandoned their pursuit to upper-level leadership roles, in male dominated corporate environment (Eagly & Carli, 2007; Ely et al., 2011).

McQueen et al., (2006); Neuman, (2007); Leedy and Ormrod, (2010) defined external validity as the degree of results to which qualitative research is comprehended or associated to other settings or environments, and the degree of threats to external validity may possibly create problems when interpreting sample data. Threats to external validity According to McQueen, et al., (2006) and Neuman, (2007) include (a) the interaction of selection and treatment, an inability to generalize beyond the participants, and (b) the interaction of setting and treatment, an inability to generalize from the setting of where the investigation is conducted to another setting.

This investigative approach utilized a case study design to ensure the collection, and analysis of different data sources provided an in-depth perspective of the participants on women in upper-level leadership roles. A methodical description of the investigative framework examined assumptions that might improve transferability (McQueen et al., 2006; Neuman, 2007; Leedy & Ormrod, 2010).

The examination of external validity related to qualitative investigative findings might apply to other situations, such as (a) aspiring young women 25-35 seeking advance to leadership positions; (b) older women 55-65 with tenure in leadership roles, (c) leaders who mentor other women advancement to leadership positions; and (d), all men and women seeking opportunities of advancement to leadership positions (McQueen et al., 2006; Leedy & Ormrod, 2010).

Data Analysis

The data analysis in this investigation focused on the examination of data collected through face-to-face interviews. The information presented by the participants was categorized and coded to determine meaningful characteristics, descriptions, and themes. Conducting an initial process of establishing word codes or short phrases from the data led to the identification of prominent characteristics and suggestive attributes of the participants and the phenomenon. Conducting a second coding process ensured the primary content and essences of the collected data. A Data clustering process accomplished required measurement and interpretation of all data collection for this investigation.

Data clustering. Data clustering is a process of grouping similar individuals, objects, language, or narratives into related groups and subcategories. Data clustering in this investigation consisted of categorized the participant data and coding words and phrases according to characteristics, descriptions, similarities, and themes. The investigative process resulted in the reliability of themes and similarities because the responses of the participants indicate various difficulties and issues encountered at different levels of leadership in Pittsburgh corporate offices. Data clustering in this investigation also consisted of grouping data to find participant perspectives and common themes (McQueen et al., 2006;

Moustakas, 1994). The steps of assembling the data collected from the face- to-face interviews into categories relevant to this investigation were of considerable value in this investigation.

Textural descriptions. The structure of the interview questions developed because of the investigation on the Labyrinth phenomenon. The content of literature review and comparison of the region in question, Pittsburgh, Pennsylvania's corporate arena, further guided the development of the interview questions. As the questions developed, a pilot study developed assuring validity. From the feedback and review of that pilot study, questions were restructured to support to the labyrinthine phenomenon studied.

The design of the questions produced dialog and provided the participant with an opportunity to express information on how life events may have affected her pursuits of executive leadership positions in Pittsburgh. For example, Participant B, D, and E described issues as follow: Women on the other hand have to justify every decision they make. Whereas the leaders (male) that hold the same positions can and do make changes to processes or decisions in leadership that women cannot. Women cannot make any decision without running it pass their superiors for approval first. This is another frustrating barrier for women in leadership no matter how successful they are.

Participant D: "I constantly prove have to my worth to my male counterparts and the workforces I lead; and sometime that included the women in my industry. I became so frustrated and so tired of feeling inadequate; I decided to leave and start my own business. Here I have the pressure to succeed. The difference is this pressure I can relate to and I know I my skills are being used to the fullest".

Participant E: women will have to scratch and claw their way to the top, however temporary. I decided that this corporate battle was not for me and if they did not want my skills and talents fine as they say, I can do bad all by myself. I left corporate America and never looked back.

Participant B: "working in the corporate arena I was in was exhausting and beyond frustrating. The pressure to perform began to affect my family and subsequently my health. I had to do something or lose everything. I worked too hard to do that; so I left. It was the best thing I had done and not sure why I waited so long to do it. I partnered (collaborated) with another business executive and we formed the company five years ago. Trials and challenges notwithstanding, we have maintained and become successful and discovering a whole new set of stressors (huge smile)".

The interview questions resulted in an exhaustive discussion of the lived experiences in Pittsburgh corporate offices. The participants in the investigation had opportunities to clarify and expound vague or abbreviated comments.

The interview questions sought were designed to provide the participants an opportunity to reflect on their experiences and perceptions of underrepresentation of female leaders in Pittsburgh corporations. Individual textural descriptions were developed based on the core themes and patterns identified through analyzing the participant responses. The analysis of the participants' perceptions and experiences resulted in an understanding of the subject studied.

Summary

Chapter 3 included discussion of the research method, design appropriateness, population, sampling, data collection, validity, and reliability, and data analysis of the current investigation. The goal of the investigation was to detail and identify areas of concern associated with the labyrinth theory to women within the Pittsburgh corporate arena. The investigation involved exploring the incongruities and concerns of the underrepresented women in executive leadership roles within the Pittsburgh corporate arena. Chapter 4 includes details the results of this investigation.

Chapter 4: Analysis and Results

This qualitative investigation involved an exploration of the experiences and perceptions of a sample of women in Pittsburgh leadership roles, with emphasis on characteristics of the labyrinthine phenomenon. An interview with participants with direct knowledge and experience within this phenomenological investigation and assessment of participants' experiences and perspectives was the chief approach to investigation. Chapter 4 includes results of data analysis, data collection, demographic data, and textural descriptions of this investigation.

Population Demographics

Prior to conducting data collection, demographic questions were added to the interview questions. Background (demographic) questions provide personal characteristics of participants (McQueen et al., 2006; Shank, 2006). Seven questions provided demographic information from each participant. The demographic questions regarded region, individual characteristics, industry, and leadership.

The region demographic established industry segments participants were in, such as public, private, or entrepreneurial in Pittsburgh, Pennsylvania. The individual characteristics refer to the participants' age, ethnicity, education, and the number individuals within the household. Age segments consisted of three categories 40–45, 45–50, and 50–55.

Ethnicity demographics were African American, Caucasian, Indian, Hispanic, and other. The education demographics consisted of associate, bachelor, master, doctorate, or other certifications or degrees. The final aspect of the individual characteristics involved the number of people in the household, including the participant, spouses, children, and parents, and significant others. The leadership demographics associated to leadership experience, years in corporate offices, and years of experience in comparable leadership roles with the Pittsburgh corporate offices.

Demographics

The targeted population of this investigation was women in midlevel leadership who sought upper-level management roles, withdrew from their pursuit of upper-level roles for entrepreneurial endeavors, or entirely separated from corporate offices. The 15 participants reported age (40–55), education, years within Pittsburgh executive offices, years pursuing or obtaining upper-level leadership roles, years within the organization, any rationales for continuing their pursuit in the immediate future, or for leaving corporate arena. Table 1 contains an overview of participants' ages, ethnicities, and levels of education. The mainstream of participants fell into an age range 40–44 comprising 60% of the population 40% of the population fell in an age range of 45–50 (see table 1).

Table 1
Demographic Composition

Code	Age	Education	Ethnicity	Position	Tenure	Family Household
L1	40	Associate's	African American	Manager	20	4
L2	40	Bachelor's	African American	Senior Associate	11	0
L3	40	Bachelor's	African American	Manager	15	3
L4	43	Master's	African American	Executive Manager	25	2
L5	44	Bachelor's	African American	Executive Director	11	1
L6	44	Master's	Asian American	Executive Director	16	2
L7	44	Associate's	Caucasian	Associate Director	16	3
L8	44	Master's	Caucasian	Executive Director	18	0
L9	44	Master's	Caucasian	Executive Director	18	1
L10	45	Master's	Caucasian	Executive Manager	18	3
L11	45	Master's	Caucasian	Executive Owner	20	4
L12	47	Associate's	Caucasian	Associate Director	24	2
L13	47	Master's	Hispanic	Executive Owner	15	1
L14	50	Bachelor's	Hispanic	Admin Manager	25	2
L15	50	Certification	Hispanic	Manager	20	2

Interviewing for the purpose of the investigation consisted of a selection of 15 participants currently in the leadership level positions or seeking upper-level position participated or is no longer pursuing leadership roles. Six out of 15 were aged 40–44, and nine out of 15 were 40–49. Participants followed a complex labyrinthine career path in an effort to achieve upper-level leadership roles in the Pittsburgh corporate, offices. The prospect of obtaining upper-level leadership in the less established age group was uncommon. In terms of education level, 13% earned associate degrees; 13% had earned Master's degrees. Twenty-six percent had earned Bachelor's degrees; 40% percent had obtained certifications through corporate developmental training equivalent to a baccalaureate degree. Additionally, no participants had earned a doctorate or indicated a need to pursue higher levels of education.

Many participants had greater than 15 years of professional experience in Pittsburgh, corporate offices, as reflected in Table 2.

Table 2
Years of Experience

Years in Pittsburgh corporate offices		Years in similar leadership roles		Years to achieve leadership roles	
Years	Participants	Years	Participants	Years	Participants
0–5	0	0–5	3	0–5	4
6–10	0	6–10	7	6–10	6
11–15	5	11–15	0	11–15	0
16–20	5	16–20	3	16–20	3
21–25	5	21–25	2	21–25	2
26–30	0	26–30	0	26–30	0

Tenure as a requirement did not affect or required for advancement or promotion. Seven of 15 participants had prior work experiences in lower level positions and were not currently pursuing advancement to upper-level positions; indicating a reluctant acceptance of the constraints within their office. Participant's inferred a concern of job stability or longevity. For example, Participant G: stated "I cannot take the risk of rocking the boat and losing my job. The market is rough out there so I endure and I am not alone I bet". Three participants revealed positions in mid-level positions for 16–20 years; five participants had been in upper level positions 6–10 years.

Each participant's decision to pursue corporate positions indicated a belief of ability to succeed in executive leadership in corporate offices. The data revealed a saturation point that established heightened tension. Of the 15 participants, thirteen expressed zero interest or desire to pursue upper-level positions beyond their current positions. Of the 15 participants, 5 had separated from corporate arena and pursued entrepreneurial endeavors. Of the 15 participants, only two remained encouraged and expressed intentions to continue their pursuits for upper-level executive positions in the Pittsburgh, Pennsylvania corporate arena. The final demographic table (Table 3) shows a breakdown of participant households. Participant households included spouses, children, elderly parent, and significant others.

Table 3
Participant Household Demographics

Participants	Number of members in the household
5	Households with one person—spouse only
4	Households with two people—spouse with a child
3	Households with three people—spouse with two children
2	Households with four people—spouse, three children, and parent
2	Households with five people—spouse, three children, and both parents

Pilot Study

The pilot study included an opportunity to review the questions in both the pre-interview survey and the in-depth interview. As the questions developed, a pilot study to assure validity. From the review and feedback of the pilot study the questions related to this investigation developed. Participants specifically discussed his or her interpretation of the questions as related to the labyrinthine phenomenon. The discussion addressed redundancy, necessity, and relevance to the nature of the investigation. Questions one, three and seven were modified and two questions were eliminated resulting in the final 16 participant questionnaire

Data Collection

The process of audiotaping for the semi-structured interviews, and the transliteration of the audiotapes identified evolving themes through an examination of the interviews. The interviews were analyzed using qualitative software that provided a means of identifying and coding the themes in the interview transcripts. (See table 4)

Table 4
Emergent Themes

Theme	Percentage
Challenges	24%
Emotions	12%
Labyrinthine Phenomenon	20%
Leadership roles	9%
Success determinants	15%
Corporation treatment	20%

Data Analysis

The data collected from the participants were analyzed to explore the labyrinthine phenomenon of women in Pittsburgh's corporate arena. The participants responded to semi-structured interview questions as a means to reflect upon the experiences women encounter. The semi-structured interview questions were developed to encourage thought and consideration from the participants to share her experiences.

Participant Profiles

A diverse cross-section of participants in the demographic profile demonstrated the significance of the lived experiences of the participant leadership roles. Participants were eager to participate and share their lives experiences about the challenges within their culturally structured corporations. Three of the participants had separated from corporate arena and established their own businesses. The following overview of participants reflects their leadership perspective, position, challenges faced, their perception of the labyrinth phenomenon and their intention to pursuit upper-level leadership roles.

Participant A. This participant felt "disillusioned, it is worse than being outsider, to some degree, no matter what I do it is dismissed then miraculously the same recommendation is made by a male counterpart and herald as novel or innovative. I seek to achieve more education or training…because I am a woman." With each promotion, she worked harder to prove she deserved to be in the position although she faced with various forms of harassment, changing of policies, and rules. The labyrinthine phenomenon, "I managed to break it, but it took me longer than my male counterparts to break it. For every position I have achieved, I have encountered the labyrinthine phenomenon. Once I have achieved the position, the rules change regarding the benefits or pay scale of the position. I was omitted from key meetings and brainstorming secessions."

Participant B. Reflected on the pushback she experienced in previous roles—whether it was age, gender, degree, or appointee-related. Pushback was definitely a challenge as well as the perception of her expertise and her ability to do the job. What she observed went beyond any glass ceiling, in her opinion the labyrinth phenomenon was in full effect with every move and sacrifice women make to advance. "Looking around the table and seeing the heavy hitters and the division in leadership. The positions held by women were the soft side of the business." Her approach to moving through the labyrinthine phenomenon has been to work harder, faster, and smarter with hope that work life balance will one day be a reality

Participant C. This participant felt empowered in occupying culturally male-dominated leadership roles, "I am more recognizable." As a woman who always has worked in male-dominated positions her biggest challenge has been racism as opposed to sexism as the president of her own company, the labyrinthine phenomenon is not a barrier.

Participant D. Participant D: reflected on her experiences as a woman occupying a male-dominated leadership role as "very hard, women are often rejected, ostracized or belittled," challenged by the changes in the Pittsburgh corporate arena, and the perceptions within the region her firm grew fast on multiple levels. Continuing, declared "discrimination continues for minority corporations". Within her firm, promotions for individuals occur often because of their merit and productivity. However, all participants indicated responses agreed the implementation of work life initiatives associated to the labyrinthine phenomenon has effected the external growth and produces challenges that continue, in the Pittsburgh corporate arena.

Participant E. Participant E: loved the work in her culturally male-dominated leadership positions however her biggest issue was partaking in the professional organizations. The presence of women is significantly lower therefore; most of her colleagues are men. Acceptance into the professional arena seldom occurred, she was, "never valued as a colleague, considered their friend or buddy, acceptance if at all was rare. Relegated to accepting jobs that no one else wanted, excelled, however, her challenges were not enough time and money to accomplish what she needed. As a female leader, educated, spouse, and mother of two, the participant said:

> I was a breaker of the glass ceiling, however, I found resistance, and difficulty maneuvering through the maze of challenges presented in leadership. The labyrinthine phenomenon is genuine, and they (management) find ways to add new twist and turns as often as they can.

Interview Questions

The next part of the data analysis was derivative of the responses from the 16 interview questions. Interview questions provided the participants' opportunities to reflect on experiences encountered, and used the participants' interpretations and words to express views and concerns. As a qualitative process of analysis of the participant responses, compiling data expressed in these results..

Interview question 1: Do you think that women have opportunities to further their knowledge and skills in the organization? Please explain. The intent of interview question 1 was to invoke a discussion of experiences and concerns about the opportunities available for women within corporate offices. The hope was that participants would openly discuss their concerns about the opportunities provided for women pursuing upper-level management positions.

Interview question 2: Are men and women offered the same training and educational benefits in your organization? This interview question was used to allow participants to describe their beliefs about if women pursued, and obtained additional skills. This question provided participants with an opportunity to reflect upon her experiences with the Pittsburg corporate offices concerning the training and educational benefits pursued by the women in the organization. The question included a discussion of the men in the organization as a contrast for the participants to discuss those training and educational benefits sought and obtained.

Interview Question 3: Do you believe that the professional growth opportunities are available for men and women? The intent of this question was to invoke a discussion from the participants about her experiences in Pittsburgh corporate offices concerning the professional growth opportunities available for women in the organization. The question included a discussion of the men in the organization as a contrast to those professional growth opportunities that men may be accepting and exploring and that women do not seek and obtain. The hope was that the participants had direct knowledge and concerns about professional growth opportunities available in the Pittsburgh corporate offices and how these opportunities affect women in the organization.

Interview question 4: Do you believe that adequate training opportunities area available for women? This interview question was asked to understand whether there are adequate training opportunities available for women. The intent of this question was to invoke a discussion about the training opportunities available for women in the organization. The intent included the hope that the participants had direct knowledge and concerns about the training opportunities available in Pittsburgh corporate offices and how these opportunities affect women in the organization.

Interview question 5: What are men's expectations of women professionals in your organization? This interview question was asked to elicit information about stereotypes, gender differences, and gender favoritism toward women in Pittsburgh corporate offices. The question was also asked to explore the societal barriers.

Interview question 6: How do other women within the Pittsburgh, Pennsylvania's corporate offices, treat women? The intent of this interview question was to elicit information about the interactions between women in the organization. The goal of this question sought to reveal aspects of societal constraints placed on women. The literature review indicated societal barriers are a part of the labyrinthine theory. Question 6 was asked to probe participants' concerns about the societal barriers women's roles educed, in the pursuit of upper-level leadership positions in Pittsburgh, Pennsylvania.

Interview question 7: What are the dynamics between men and women in the organization? This interview question was used to provoke a discussion about the diverse dynamics, working relationship, and differences between men and women. The anticipation was that each participant would discuss the experiences and concerns of women in Pittsburgh's corporate arena regarding the attributes of leadership.

Interview question 8: Do you feel that your organization has been effective in employing and retaining women? Explain. This question was the catalyst for a discussion of if retention of qualified women is a concern for Pittsburgh corporate offices. The data suggested additional reasons women may not be advancing in the organization or may not remain at the Pittsburgh corporate offices.

Interview question 9: Describe the barriers that you have encountered during your career. This question was asked to bring about discussions about leadership attributes asociated to gender differences in the Pittsburgh corporate arena and how these attributes contributed to the disparity of women in upper level leadership roles. Research concurred with participant beliefs that gender differences played a significant part in gender biases and stereotypes.

Interview question 10: How did you deal with the barriers that you have encountered during your career? This question was used to understand the differences in barriers observed for women. The idea was for the participants to discuss barriers encountered during her career progress in hope that they would provide relevant information for how they positively and constructively viewed those barriers they encountered. Participants believed that barriers were tantamount to stereotypes and are a part of the societal norm for any organization. Participants further agreed that the objective would be to review the barriers as a positive, constructive attribute that aided women to perform in an outstanding manner.

Interview question 11: Do you think that men and women face similar barriers throughout their careers? The intent of this question was to obtain information about participant's beliefs and concerns for women concerning the barriers women faced. In addition, if women faced barriers attempting to enter into the senior leadership roles in the Pittsburgh corporate arena was vastly different from those barriers faced by men.

Interview question 12: How has the culture influenced the career of women in your organization? The question's intent was to examine similarities of perspectives and perceptions of men and women that the organizational culture may have on the advancement of women in the organization. The participants were management level executives in the Pittsburgh corporate arena.

Interview question 13: What role do informal power structures play in the organization? The intent of this question was to solicit discussions on the influence informal power structures had on the progress of women. Research evidence indicates that women have concerns regarding the varying networking structures and powers in the corporate arenas that do not affect male colleagues (Eagly & Carli, 2007). The data Eagly and Carli (2007) presented indicates women are aware or concerned with the maze like obstacles, and informal power struggles completely comprehending the influence these power struggles have on the organizational culture and on the career advancement of women in the organization.

Interview question 14: What are some factors that you feel may limit women's potential in leadership positions? The intent of this question was to obtain information about the possible commonalities in participant experiences. The objective was to offer data and information to other individuals aspiring to obtain upper level management positions.

Interview question 15: Do you have a mentor? How has this mentorship affected your career? The intent of interview question 15 was to gain an understanding of the participants' views of mentoring, and possible influential growth or career guidance provided.

Interview question 16: Despite all your training, do you believe you still can climb the corporate ladder? Interview question 16 provided an opportunity for the participants to express their intent to continue their pursuit to advance to upper levels of leadership in Pittsburgh's corporate arena. Prompting a response of goals based on perception of ability, expectations imposed whether corporate or self, training and tenure with regard to future probabilities.

Findings and Emerging Themes

The complexity of data analysis involved the compilation of intricate data. Analysis of the women (40–55), in Pittsburgh corporate offices experiences permitted the research to identify common themes and patterns. A prudent assessment process of inductive reasoning applied to the responses of the open-ended survey to develop distinct structural descriptions. Distinct structural descriptions aided in the explanation of participants' personal concerns and beliefs.

Analyzing the interview data led to distinctive themes regarding the experiences of the labyrinthine phenomenon. The findings resulted in an understanding of the participants' experiences and knowledge gained from the labyrinthine phenomenon.

Core themes emerged from the discussions of experiences, and the interpretation of these discussions resulted in descriptive meanings reflective and characteristic of the group. An examination of participant reactions provided comprehension of the current phenomenon. The process of assessing commonalities preserves the phenomenon, provides evaluation of the current phenomenon, enables longevity of the phenomenon and increases the core of credibility associated with the phenomenon.

Only relevant and consistent participant responses to the investigation included saturation of the hypothesis of this investigation.

- R1. What barriers do women in Pittsburgh, Pennsylvania, corporate offices perceive as inhibiting their promotion in the workplace?
- R2. What are the reasons women are leaving Pittsburgh, Pennsylvania, corporate offices, and abandoning the pursuit of executive leadership roles?

From 16 interview questions, core themes were developed. The categorized themes are treatment from corporate leadership, labyrinthine phenomenon, opportunities available, professional knowledge, skills, and abilities, recruitment, and retention of women, gender versus leadership attributes and style, emotions, and separation, personal desires to excel, departure from the corporate arena, and mentorship.

The major themes that were identified indicate specific reasons women may be taking the approach to available opportunities of advancement. Treatment from corporate leadership, labyrinthine phenomenon, opportunities available, professional knowledge, skills, and abilities, recruitment, and retention of women, gender versus leadership attributes, and style, emotions, and separation, and personal desires to excel, departure, and mentorship.

Treatment from corporate leadership. Nine of the respondents believed the major barriers were associated to the treatment of women executives. This treatment they considered lopsided and unfair; sighting that their male colleagues receive opportunities of advancement not given to women. Especially noted was the link between barriers and treatment women receive after returning to corporate arena post childbirth or educational sabbaticals. Some of the personal reasons included a belief that they (women) cannot devote the time necessary, women cannot perform competitively or sufficiently, women lack the stamina for aggressive opportunities, or leadership fear women cannot succeed and will humiliate the organization in their failure. As stated by Participant 9:

> As a result of the treatment from leaders most women have not moved forward because they are comfortable where they are. Leadership continues to limit opportunities for women and create unwarranted hurdles and obstacles to advance. The fact they [leadership] prevents [women] or block our efforts is a valid concern that places unwarranted pressures. If offered an opportunity greater, expectations apply to those (women) who take on roles and responsibilities, and the demands are astonishingly rigid.

More than half thirteen of the respondents vehemently opposed the idea of pursuing opportunities of advancement. As indicated by Participant C;

> I will never seek a male-dominated assignment or position; I have watched too many women truly traumatized by overwhelming pressures and demanding expectations never seen or applied to men. Furthermore, I am not convinced women here want to take on the [same] challenges or responsibilities as men because of the imposed barriers. No, I do not wish to be in the cross-hairs of my bosses like that ever!

Participant B noted that "women do not have the same opportunities as men without facing continual hurdles and obstacles to conquer for advancement." In many cases these hurdles change without notices and new obstacle apply with or at each level of advancement.

Labyrinthine phenomenon. Twelve of the participants believed that women in their industries suffer a different form of discrimination because of life events and penalized for taking time to address family needs or to advance, personal educational skills. The labyrinthine phenomenon is indicative of women who face difficulties because they have different work-life needs and responsibilities. The barriers that prevent women from engaging executives and stakeholders stem from a perspective that women possess a single-minded focus not associated to business. As women pursue the necessities of life events (childbearing, family needs, education, etc.); when women return to the workforce a different level of competency and revealed expectation. Further responses also indicated the issues persist, as do the perceptions of leadership that reflects a perception about a woman's focus is on family needs not business. Participant D replied, "I think women are not considered because the perception is that we are 'little Suzie homemakers' with family obligations that preoccupy our existence and the only things we can do is take care of kids and cook dinner"

Twelve of the participants believed opportunities to 'schmooze' with perspective clientele are not readily available or offered to women. As indicated by Participant D "Advance notices of opportunities are circulated to every male manager and division leader first. By the time women find out about the opportunity the position is filled or requirements changed." Further discussion indicated that most of the information received was secondhand, and if women express an interest in participating, women are not necessarily denied inasmuch as women discouraged not to pursue the opportunity in one manner or another. "Either way," Participant D continued, "the resulting pressure is great."

Professional knowledge, skills, and abilities. Twelve of the respondents believed that most women are suffering because of lack of knowledge or ability to perform ad their male colleagues. Participant K said:

> It is sad I know of many women who feel threatened about pursuing additional training and education. Those who have stopped working to have children have met with significant difficulties also. I know because I am one who has stopped working twice for my blessed events and the only regret are

the imposed limitations the industry has applied because of the opinions my abilities.

Participant G stated, "In my corporation in addition to the limitations, we encounter there are travel issues. Many women here are unwilling to travel as men and in an effort to seek promotion and therefore do not pursue opportunities of advancement."

Five of 15 participants believed a lack of flexibility for women at the organization exists. The long work hours and too much time spent physically in the office prompted women not to be as flexible as men did. One of the many barriers is the fear of taking a hiatus to advance studies or handle family needs also prevent women from professionally advancing. Participant 4 responded:

I for one have reached a point in my life where long hours are no longer desirable. I also know that in this company, depending on the level of management women expected to spend lengthy hours in the office or field. Advancing any further would present problems I do not have time to face. The next opportunity I seek is to make a move toward the door. Essentially, I feel like this, if I take the time to build my knowledge, it will not be appreciated or used properly, so why bother.

Thirty percent sought every opportunity to advance, though, often denied. Participant F expounded:

It seems the more I try to advance the more obstacles are placed and I am denied advancement. I have been told to reach certain levels I must maintain a particular training or level of certification, once accomplished consideration would be given, only to find out the position is no longer available.

Recruitment and retention. The analysis of the transcribed interviews revealed that the participants responded as a two-part analysis on the discussion of recruiting efforts ranging from organizations doing an excellent job, a very good job, a good job or not doing a good job of their recruiting efforts.

Seven participants indicated that the leaders at the Pittsburgh corporate arena do an excellent job in their recruiting efforts. As stated by Participant J, "There is nothing specific to the recruitment or retention process that my industry has established however, this does not mean that women are highly sought after or retained either."

Ten participants suggested that the leaders at their level of operations in Pittsburgh, corporate office do a very good job in their recruiting efforts and 20% ranked the recruiting efforts as lacking or poor. Further analysis of the participant transcripts revealed retention of qualified women was a concern for at the offices of Pittsburgh, corporate arena.

The major themes and corresponding participant responses emerged suggested additional reasons women may not be advancing or may remain in the Pittsburg corporate arena. 10 of 15 participants indicated retention as a cultural issue as suggested by Participant K, "The workforce philosophy in Pittsburgh, and our nation has to include women, recruit and retain talented women. However, organizations still impose limitations or have established specific gender based requirements for advancement."

10 of the 15 participants indicated retention of women in upper management was not necessarily a high priority. As suggested by Participant C, "women usually do not remain in these positions; they seem to be in constant movement from one corporate office or position to another." Retention and tenure in those positions are much lower for women than men.

Gender versus leadership attributes and style. The major theme of the participant suggested gender difference and required attributes was a very important factor for a leader. Five of the participants indicated that prescribe attributes and style of leadership remained masculine and provided little encouragement toward women in leadership roles. Participant F stated, "I wish I had had someone who could have taken me by the hand and said do this not that as I was coming along." Participant I stated:

> Surrounded by men, I had no idea there was a difference in requirements or styles until I entered the Pittsburgh, Pennsylvania, corporate arena. Until then my perspective was negative against women's complaints until I ran into

them. Now I wish I had the insight and guidance necessary to make this battle a bit easier. Let us just say I am learning there is a marked difference between men and women in Pittsburgh's corporate arena.

Emotions and separation. Participants expressed specific feelings associated to occupying culturally male-dominated roles. 8 of 15 participants did not feel appreciated by their organizations. The lack of significance led to a decision to pursue outside opportunities. Participant G stated, "I do not feel appreciated in my organization. I definitely do not feel accepted as a knowledgeable woman capable of leading an organization."

10 of 15 participants expressed feelings of separation in addition to the emotional stressors related to women in leadership. Participant I expressed:

How do you explain sitting in a room filled with leaders and you're the only women at the table? The discussions are one-sided and it is apparent you are there only to appease law requirements. You are invisible, never called upon or acknowledge, and have no voice. It is the ultimate separation.

Participants F tearfully recalled moments when her child was ill requiring that she leave early hearing an insensitive comment as she exited: "What, he's sick again." However, she noted, when my male colleagues' leave to pick up a sick child, comments herald him as a great dad. Continuing she declared, "in this region, no one knows how emotionally trying and disturbing it can be in the corporate arenas accept another woman." The professionalism the women in the Pittsburgh corporate arena continually seek to bring the best of their personal and professional lives to the office; only to be emotionally discouraged with every effort to achieve success.

Participant C who expressed her dismay that her family cannot rely on her discussed another emotional aspect woman in the Pittsburg corporate arena. "It is like juggling chainsaws sometimes trying to find the time to be with my family and in the office too. The constraints of my current position has only served to move me further away from my family." Participant B stated her position has placed great strain on her family as she stated:

> Travel requirements alone have me on the road (especially during peak seasons) an estimated two to three months out the year. I cannot make those times at home coincide with key dates like recitals and picture day. My salary is great, but my family is not happy and I will have to make a decision very soon just how much more I can put on them.

The participants further indicated that their male colleagues did not hesitate to make them aware of their (women) decision to accept roles that included travel. However, "the major difference between the men and the women in this region was the male colleagues exchange assignments with other male colleagues" (Participant B).

Eagly and Carli (2007) challenged leadership to revisit the complexities labyrinthine obstacles women encounter in their pursuit to executive leadership in corporate arenas. Hogue (2010) challenged the idea of accomplishing equality in the Pittsburgh corporate arena. These challenges emphatically argue in addition to participant responses, the complexities, and obstacles of work experiences women encounter persist and multifaceted (Hogue, 2010).

Personal development. The Pittsburgh corporate arena has seen an increase of women in the corporate arena (Catalyst, 2011). However, the workplace environment imposes challenges of advancement and equality for women (Haney, 2010). Three participants in this investigation expressed their desires to excel in the Pittsburgh corporate arena however difficult the path or requirements were. For example, Participant L expressed "I seek to know everything. With hope, the more I know the greater influence I will have and I can climb the ladder to success." Conversely, Participant J's discussion expressed her realistic view of women advancing in the Pittsburgh corporate arena:

> Right now we are not making much headway. However, I think we will make it one day it will rely on how much effort we [women] make to reach the top. I think if women continue to seek upper level leadership, we will excel beyond

expectation; if we can survive the relentless obstacles and torturous barriers, imposed on us.

13 out of 15 participants acknowledged they have not reached the levels of leadership in their careers, and desires remain unchanged, whether they continue pursuit for upper-level management.

Five participants expressed satisfaction with their current position or status as indicated by Participant N, who declared:

I think I have done an incredible thing just reaching this level of management. Do not get me wrong, advancement is an issue for us [women] in Pittsburgh, and I know rocking the boat is not a good thing in this region. So obtaining the level of success that keeps management off my back is acceptable; for now. I will eventually advance, just not now, and that is with me.

The responses of the participant served to validate the premise of this research results that significant labyrinthine barriers remain and continue to hinder advancement for women in the Pittsburgh corporate arena (Berry & Frank, 2010; Davis et al., 2010; Haney, 2010). If women in the Pittsburgh corporate arena seek to obtain equality in the male-dominated workplace, a degree of adaptability required.

According to Eagly and Carli (2007), this adaptability requires women to develop a greater sense of assertiveness, proficiency, confidence, and assertiveness. The premise that the culture in the Pittsburg corporate arena has changed as women enhance their abilities, education, personalities, and workplace participation is satisfied by the current invesitgation as participants revealed continuing efforts have not satisfied the approach or support of women's ascension to the executive office.

Departure. The intense pressure and continual changes for many women in leadership has prompted their departure from the Pittsburgh corporate arena. Of the 15 participants of this investigation, five participates departed the corporate office to pursue other business endeavors or have withdrawn from the corporate arena entirely (Greenwald, 2006). Participant K stated:

I fought too hard to gain the knowledge and leadership abilities to make a difference. I was one or should say I am one of those who actually thought my skills would open doors and that times would allow a strong women to lead…not the case at all.

Participant D stated:

I struggled for 6 years to gain ground and most of that time was spent in trying to maintain what I have accomplished. I watched the male colleagues excelled pass me who possessed little or no knowledge. Finally, I had enough and started my own enterprise. I have successfully run my company for 12 years now applying all my knowledge and my staff appreciates.

Participant F proclaimed:

I simply had enough of the foolishness. I was suffering, my family was suffering, and the battles in the office were relentless. I decided this is not for me and withdrew from the Pittsburgh, Pennsylvania business offices. I work for me now and we (family) are happier than ever.

Leadership behaviors in the Pittsburgh's corporate arena characteristically have influenced women presence to the extent gender imposed differences dictate toward women in the workplace. Research studies conclude that characteristics such as motive, personality traits, perceived socio-cultural skills, embedded in the societal cultures has influenced leadership behavior and negatively influenced the progress of women in Pittsburgh, Pennsylvania (Davis et al., 2010).

Mentoring. Mentoring had a significant influence to women in the Pittsburgh corporate arena. 13 of 15 participants welcomed mentorship regardless of gender. Participant C stated, "I believe mentoring is vital to every woman seeking to advance in business and it does not matter if the mentoring comes for a man or a woman. If the mentoring is encouraging, informative and uplifting it is valuable." Participant I:

I'll take sound guidance anytime and savvy business woman looks for guidance everywhere and from everyone. The trick is to decipher between the good, the bad and the ugly; knowing that even the ugliest of advice is beneficial if applied properly.

Zahidi and Ibarra (2010) declared mentoring serves as a great benefit in addition to education and human talent. Mentoring from corporate leadership is the most valuable resource and development tool for women. Of the participants surveyed, five looked only to women as mentors.

Within this investigative research, the participants further validate the premise expressing the benefit of acquiring a mentor who could relate to their pursuit to ascend the corporate ladder. Participant K stated

There is nothing like having a non-judgmental sounding board to bounce ideas off. I did not realize how lost I was until I connected with her [mentor]. Having access to unbiased, professional who has endured the ever changing aspects of this region changed my perspective and approach of my leadership endeavors."

Participant C indicated mentoring is valuable:

If you do not have a mentor, every professional woman should develop a mentor relationship, and not just from other women in the industry. I think we (women) can benefit from a good mentor and should not limit our options. We should consider both male and female mentors.

Outliers

The survey revealed three outliers. The first outlier, one participant expressed zero affects from the labyrinthine phenomenon imposed within their organization, and believed that life events did not presented issues for women in leadership. Participant O stated

I elected to hold off having children so therefore I do not have many issues other women may encounter. However, there are something's just not worth fighting. As long as the compensation is adequate for the work, and I can perform that is good enough for me. The only battle I wish to engage in is the battle to retire in peace one day.

From the perspective of other participant responses was not realistic or representative of the obstacles women encounter. The realities associated to women enduring unwarranted obstacles, agonizing twist and unpredictable turns associated with obligatory requirements to advance are tangible and not imagined.

The second outlier revealed in this survey was one participant believed women were not victims of discrimination, male or otherwise. This participant blamed women for their failure to succeed and not having the backbone to stand up to fierce competition. Participant N stated

> If women want to advance, they should be prepared for battle and not expect things to be handed to them from their colleagues. Frankly, I believe we have given men too much credit and authority and it is time to stop whining and take it back!

This outlier is indicative of a sticky floor syndrome rather than a labyrinthine phenomenon. In expression, the participant places the lack of advancement in corporate offices squarely on the shoulders of women. Whereas a vast perception of the labyrinth phenomenon from the participants as indicative of unwarranted actions that prevent and are the overall cause of the lack of advancement in corporate offices.

The third outlier revealed two participants C and F categorically expressed intent to pursue upper-level roles no matter what challenges they encounter. One response to question 16 ("Despite all your training, do you believe you can still climb the corporate ladder?") was:

> Absolutely, I plan to run this organization someday and have told them as much. I think if I continue what I am doing and remain knowledgeable, I will make it someday. Please understand I know it is not going to be easy, hell, it is not easy now, but if I stay the course I believe I shall prevail.

This disconfirming outlier was contrary to the participants perspectives of this investigation. The views presented these two participants conveyed reflected defiance, resilience and determination to succeed. A counter perspective is the challenges the participants encounter daily reflected acts of survival rather than defiance. Requiring women in corporate settings to make decisions or take actions that will sustain employment or retain their current positions. Additionally according to Eagly and Carli (2007), the challenges women encounter in their pursuit to ascend the corporate ladder become somewhat navigable with a supportive mentor.

Summary

The purpose of this qualitative investigation: Women and the Labyrinth theory: Myths and Realities at the Corporate Level in Pittsburgh sought to examine the perceptions of 15 women ages 40–55, in Pittsburgh corporate offices. The goal of the research investigation sought to prove or refute and expound on the labyrinthine phenomenological experiences and review how this phenomenon affected the advancement of women into upper-level leadership positions. The participants were current Pittsburgh corporate management level members (40–55). In association with the labyrinthine phenomenon sought to add to the context of knowledge of women in corporate offices an examination of the perceptions and concerns of women in corporate offices with the Pittsburgh region

Chapter 4 included detailed information on data collection, data analysis, and the findings. Chapter 5 includes conclusions, emerging themes, implications, the significance of the investigation, and recommendations for leaders and future research. An assessment of collected data formulated the conclusion presented by participant responses. Based on the data responses, women in the corporate arena in Pittsburg perceive the labyrinthine phenomenon is factual.

The organizations within the Pittsburgh corporate arena present many hindrances and obstacles indicative of the labyrinthine phenomenon. The perspective of this labyrinthine phenomenon is characteristic of intricate pathways; tortuous twists and sudden blind stops. Eagly and Carli (2007) applied this phenomenon as conditions encountered when women return to the workplace. The labyrinthine phenomenon begins an unexpected journey of twist, turns, and abrupt obstacles that hinder or stop progress entirely in the corporate arena.

Two research questions established foundation to prove the premise of the labyrinthine phenomenon in the Pittsburg corporate arena. The research questions were as follows: What barriers do women in the Pittsburgh corporate arena perceive as inhibiting their promotion in the workplace? What are the reasons women are leaving Pittsburgh corporate offices, and abandoning the pursuit of executive leadership roles? From the investigation of these questions, six emerging themes identified treatment by corporation, success determinants, leadership roles, labyrinthine phenomenon, emotions, and challenges. Five subthemes identified family obligations, gender bias, stress, and loneliness.

Research findings from the themes identified characteristics of (a) gender bias, (b) dismissive behavior toward women in leadership roles, (c) unwarranted leadership roles, (d) double standards of family obligation, and (e) refusal to integrate the work-life leadership models.

Examining the emerging themes of this research investigation allowed to the participants to expound on their shared experiences and presumptions of the characteristics of gender bias, dismissive behaviors toward women holding culturally male-dominated leadership roles. This investigative research promoted aspects of future leadership models and perspectives for further research into the labyrinthine phenomenon. Further investigation and adoption of new leadership models may improve an organization-wide workplace relationship. For example, implementing work-life initiatives that embrace and support life events would benefit organizations globally. Initiatives such as this would improve workforce and workplace relations; possibly enhance productivity, therefore increasing corporate revenue. Future research focusing on the labyrinthine phenomenon that included men and a broader investigative analysis of the women who exit Pittsburgh, corporate arena possibly could broaden the perspectives of corporate leadership's comprehension on constructive collaborative agendas that build gender relations within the organizations.

This labyrinthine phenomenological research investigation concluded that 13 of the participants were currently experiencing or had experienced various degrees of labyrinthine effects resulting from life events and subsequent return to the corporate arena. Two of the women interviewed expressed no concern or effects from the labyrinthine phenomenon. In consideration and based on the findings of this investigation a recommendation of future research initiatives and leadership models that may affect positive changes for women in the workplace and improve the working experience and relations on every level of business operations.

Chapter 5: Conclusions and Recommendations

The specific problem is that ever-changing barriers known as labyrinthine phenomenon becomes complex by life events or tortious twists associated with labyrinth phenomenon. This labyrinthine phenomenon's hinders a woman's progress from attaining positions of leadership in Pittsburgh's corporate arena. Conflict theory, role congruity and social roles theories of were the theoretical perspectives guiding this investigation. A face-to-face process of interviewing to collect the data, and an interpretation of text along in conjunction with the van Kaam method (McQueen et al., 2006; Moustakas, 1994; Shank, 2006) to analyze the phenomenological data asociated to the gender bias experienced by women who occupied senior leadership roles within the utilities industry.

Findings and Interpretations of the Data

In Chapter 4, six main themes and five sub-themes were identified as a result of the interviews and the analysis of data using Microsoft Excel 2010 Analysis ToolPak data analysis software. The six main themes identified the treatment in Pittsburg, corporation arena as challenges each woman faced in her leadership role. The success determinants of how the women sustained their leadership positions. The struggles of women in their leadership roles associated to perception, credibility, and emotions associated to working in a male-dominated leadership role. In addition how women encountered barriers and bias associated with the labyrinthine phenomenon and the effect on their leadership. The following section provides an overview of these investigative results.

Investigative Results

Investigative results, revealed six main themes, and five subthemes emerged from the aproach. The themes emerged from the data collected and analyzed using an interpretation of text and the van Kaam method. The interpretation of text identified the emerging themes to the point of saturation. The point of saturation occurred when the data analysis no longer revealed new information (McQueen et al., 2006; Shank, 2006). Table 4 contains highlights of the significance of the themes as associated to participant responses.

Theme 1: The treatment by corporations. Grounded on the data analysis, as women occupied male-dominated leadership roles corporations in Pittsburgh had difficulty adjusting to women in leadership. This difficulty often led to negative treatment to women in leadership roles. Previous literature highlighted the norms and practices of corporations (Berry & Franks, 2010). Women in Pittsburgh, corporate present a disparate with leadership, a paradigm traditionally defined in a masculine context. Therefore, women are in disparaging situations and perceived as incapable for leadership (Eagly & Carli, 2007).

The investigation revealed corporations within the Pittsburgh corporate arena demonstrated a lack of preventative action against the labyrinthine phenomenon occurrences. Respondents provided numerous labyrinthine encounters in their corporate offices. According to Participant M, some female experiences included men refusing to perform under women leadership, to the extent of resigning from positions supervised by women:

> "I fought to get a position as lead manager; the tension was palpable during the introductions. 48 hours later, I was reassigned because 85% [all male] of the staff refused or threatened to resign if I remained lead. I was summarily demoted and told this is why we don't place people like you in these positions.

Participant

These lived experiences were subversive and emotionally draining actions such as exclusion from meetings, receipt of misinformation or failure to produce pertinent information, and unfair compensation; in addition participants reported a failure in services performed.

Participants C, G, H, and M, considered these actions as subversive and emotionally draining. For example, Participant G reported:

> I ran this intricate project that required team cooperation. During meetings, the team reported tasks accomplished or almost met. When final aspect were due, I discovered that most of the task were not completed, reports were altered to reflect I knew the status and failed to offer solutions to

satisfy the task. It destroyed my confidence, and took my trust away. They placed another lead in command; I was demoted to second in command only because I had evidence to support the works I had done. That did not correct the deliberate sabotage of a project because I am a woman.

Perceptions and behavior of male leaders who do not believe women should be in roles of leadership continues to hinder the ascension to upper-level leadership (Eagly & Carli, 2007). In the pursuit of leadership, many participants experienced demeaning and offensive treatment. Participants also revealed a flawed perception of their abilities to perform tasks associated with leadership.

Participant B:

Shortly after my return to the work place, I noticed I was excluded from key meetings with clientele. At first, I thought it was because of prior scheduling but found out they no longer considered me a key negotiator in client relations. The explanation given, I no longer possessed the stamina or ability to do the work. My boss added, besides, being eliminated means more time to spend with my family and cook that dinner.

Participant G discussed the emotional challenges she encountered stating:

Having my sons' was a blessing however the workplace made it seem like a curse. When I returned to work, I was relegated to an administrative manager. Apparently, have children renders women to a level of incompetency that prevents them from doing anything challenging. I fought for months to regain my prior position their response; they eliminated my position. It was demeaning and created an intolerable environment for me. I sought employment elsewhere but could not rely on good recommendations from the firm.

Participants B, C, G, H, M, and I reported these emotional, environmental perceptions were acts or actions associated with childbearing and addressing family needs. These social barriers and socio-cultural practices create conflict in the roles of leadership for women. Role conflict (Lynch, 2007) emerges when diverse expectations interrupt simultaneously, resulting in difference for the individual who attempts actively to combine dissimilar roles (Biddle & Thomas, 1979).

The consistent stereotypical behavior such as this created uncomfortable, tensioned filled environments for women pursuing leadership roles. The presence of women in leadership challenges men in leadership (Euwema, Wendt, & Van Emmerik, 2007; Greenwald, 2006) to implement changes within the Pittsburgh corporate arena. Participant A discussed her emotional state following her attempt to enter the Pittsburgh corporate arena:

> My family relocated to Pittsburgh when my husband accepted a surgical position. Before then, I was in executive management. I sought positions here [Pittsburgh] and found resistance. Some interviews were ridiculous asking me if I knew where I was now, indicating the best he could do was placing me under junior management, and doubted how I would fit into their expectations. Others [corporations] did not respond at all. Therefore, I decided to invest in myself and use my talents elsewhere. I am working on a business plan and design to launch my own company.

Therefore, women encounter an escalation of challenges and increased resistance against women pursuing upper-level leadership. Cultural stereotypes (Eagly & Sczesny, 2009) for women in the Pittsburgh corporate arena often reflected perceptions of women lacking the ability to perform important leadership roles. These perceptions add to the barriers encountered by women pursuing roles with important power and authority. Eagly and Sczesny's (2009) research on cultural masculinity stereotypes dominating femininity in organizations. Positing organizations within a masculine cultural environment think males are suited for decision-making leadership positions.

Although women are less desirable in leadership roles because of compassion and empathy that interferes with corporate decision making (Eagly & Sczesny, 2009). As stated by Participant O, "Moving up the corporate ladder posed many obstacles for career, the further I went the more roadblocks, punitive treatment, and inequality I encountered."

Theme 2: Barriers and challenges. Briggs et al. (2011) identified organizational barriers as gender role assumptions, lack of national policy, rigid schedules, lack of management support and corporate culture. These barriers work in conjunction preventing organizations from successfully developing family supported environments (Van den Steen, 2010). A significant number of participants, 12 out of 15, cited perceptions as a challenge in the occupation of male dominant leadership roles. Another perspective associated to these organizational barriers conducted by Savage-Austin and Honeycutt, discussed organizational barriers as they relate to servant leadership theory. Postulating the philosophy of servant leadership addressed the different way of understanding the responsibility of leadership that acts as a steward over his or her area of responsibility. Organizational leaders assume the attitude, roles, and services of leaders and followers in his or her socio-cultural environments. In this sense, Van den Steen (2010) declared organizational barriers operating under the theory of servant leadership unintentionally operate in a sense of shared values and beliefs that influence culture and performance negatively for women in the corporate arena. The perception that women in the Pittsburgh corporate arena lacked the ability or were unfit to lead continues to create disparity in the workplace (Greenwald et al., 2006). Stereotypically, perceives men as natural leaders whereas women are homemakers, incapable of performing beyond a secretary level of competency and therefore unfit to lead (Davis et al., 2010; Distelhorst, 2005; Eagly, 2007).

During the interviews, participants discussed enduring experiences of dismissal by their male colleagues, lack of acknowledgment, validation, and being invisible in meetings. Participant B reported:

> I submitted recommendations for change that were summarily dismissed. Not, one month later the same recommendations emerged from a male colleague. The identical recommendations were presented, in the exact format (probably on the same paper—chuckling); his

recommendations were accepted and viewed a success process by upper level management.

This is a continual challenge of the biases women in the Pittsburgh corporate offices encounter. Participants noted, though, they possessed established records of accomplishment women leaders had to rely on their male colleagues to provide credibility, and validation of their leadership acuity. Without support of their male colleagues, women's ascension to upper-level leadership roles and stereotypical perceptions continue to hinder advancement.

Leadership stereotypes placed participants in unwarranted and challenging leadership roles to prove fitness to lead. Resulting in the acceptance or volunteering of undesirable roles requiring lengthy hours to perform. In essence, women found their leadership roles in positions rejected by their male colleagues. Participant D recalled offers for project leadership roles that several male colleagues turned down, stating, "we [upper level] asked 30 people, and she was the only one who said yes noting the prestigious jobs are immediately taken or held by men. Only women held those positions perceived insignificant, difficult, or unsuitable for male leadership."

Though the workplace has changed and recent statics indicate a three percent (3%) increase in the presence of women in corporate America (Catalyst, 2012) there remain several basic ideologies in the Pittsburgh corporate arena hindering professional advancement and equality for women (Haney, 2010). The following are ideological-related professional developmental difficulties women encounter:

- Sexual harassment and sexism in the workplace
- Socio-cultural gender biases that begin at childhood
- Labyrinthine phenomenon and lack of support for educational pursuits, child rearing, and family obligations
- Competition and divisiveness between women caused by fewer positions available in the workplace
- Lack of organizational integrity, or consistency of character in actions, flawed communication
- Gender related leader vision, live core values

- Challenge of lack of respect, ability, appreciation, faithfulness to service
- Lack of devotion, loyalty, and respect toward women

The investigative approach includes a subtheme perception that women are nurturers, caregivers, and primarily focused on having babies (Eagly & Carli, 2007, 2008; Eagly & Sczesny, 2009) hindering transition and advancement up the corporate ladder. Of the two hundred forty-six pages of transcribed interviews, 10 of the participants expressed notable differences in advancement, male colleagues advanced five to ten years sooner than women did. The continual expectation that women are homebodies with a primarily goal is to conceive and bear children remains a hurdle women much conquer. Stereotypically, the view of the role of working women was as stay-at-home household managers, rearing children as the support of the family. Kwolek-Folland (2007) declared women have been dominated the eighteenth century, in the United States. The domination of women began with the development of services as part of the United States economy. Women began to work as domestic workers, provided services, such as nursing, millinery dressmakers, and eventual clerical, and retailing workers by the nineteenth century. As women ventured beyond the home to start their professions, businesses were small, labor-intensive operations typically slow growing and service orientated. Women who pursued entrepreneurial endeavors were considered divorced, widowed, or at home with small children, or starting businesses out of financial necessity (Davis et al., 2010). These stereotypical beliefs present challenges and continue hindering women pursuing professional advancement in the Pittsburgh corporate arena.

These challenges require women to defend their abilities and competency to advance as discussed by 12 of the Participants. Participant A recalled defending her ability as going beyond capability or skill to defending her plans for parenthood as the interviewer (male) asked, "do you have plans to have children? If so, why would we hire you only knowing we would have to replace you when you get pregnancy in the near future?" Participant E expressed the following, "despite my age, the perception remains only with a twist." Continuing, the participant said:

I am no longer asked if I plan to have children, in a conventional manner. I am asked, what is your position on adoption or foster parenting and do, you have plans to do so? My response is a resounding NO, coupled with laughter.

The tonality of perceptions does not change, in fact evolves into another level of discrimination that women encounter. Suggesting according to Davis et al. (2010) the perception of professional women populating these environments, past, and present are shaped by the ideas of domestic labor and services.

The investigation further revealed the inflexibility of corporations in the Pittsburgh arena leaving few opportunities for those women who had major responsibilities for raiding young children. Participant C recalled the harsh treatment she encountered following a simple mistake:

The mistake was a minor infringement. My supervisor called me incompetent, a waste of time and energy, and a mistake. Continuing he suggested that I should have stayed home. It is apparent you are more suited to run your home than this office. My evaluation later that month fell from met and above satisfactory to unsatisfactory on every level. Further sanctions resulted in probation for six month."

A previous research by Distelhorst (2005), and current studies (Corea, Guaya, & Lackerb, 2008; Amatucci & Crawley, 2011) concurs that imposed perceptions that women place family first, and schedules that are inflexible to work requirements and schedules. This rigidity creates the conflict women in leadership face because of gender differences and leadership roles

Participant responses associated with the Pittsburgh, Pennsylvania corporate arena further revealed an expectation that women are home with children prompted personal questions about pregnancy and family planning in the context of job or project assignments. "The men advised that I could not be promoted to a specific level because I would be leaving to have babies, at least that was their assumption." This perceived expectation of inflexibility further enhanced emotional fear and frustration for women leadership Pittsburgh, Pennsylvania (Corea, Guaya, & Lackerb,

2008; Amatucci & Crawley, 2011). Participant D reflected on the degree of tension that seemed to emerge over her division;

> My director made it known that the position we held did not provided hiatus opportunities [non-specific educational endeavors or maternity leave] we were hired to for a specific task and nothing more. However, our male colleagues were often off on "assignment" later revealed as training opts for advancement. If we discovered information about an outside training session, the requirements to attend would change".

The continuing perceived biasness by the respondents prompted a considerable number of participants to separate from the established corporate offices to establish their own company endeavors and implement their skills (Eagly et al., 2007; Corea, Guaya, & Lackerb, 2008; Amatucci & Crawley, 2011). Five of 15 participants surveyed established company operations that enabled them, function in the capacity associated to the level of skills, to implement the leadership role as envisioned, and allowed the flexibility desired to be with family without guilt or reservation. As stated by Participant D "The higher you go, the more inflexibility women encounter. Unfortunately, most industries or corporations do not offer flex hours that allow spending time with their family."

The inability and inflexibility women leaders in Pittsburgh corporate offices enhanced the levels of stress and tension. This created challenges as women attempted to establish a balance between family and the workplace. Eight participants noted their dismay and frustration associated to efforts to find balance for the passions of their lives. For example, Participant H discussed "As someone who thrives on challenge I find it difficult some days to endure the level of stress related to my profession. I absolutely love what I do, but they (male leadership) make it ugly at times." However, Participant E sees things differently as she declared:

> I am here for a reason and they just have to get over themselves. The fighter in me has not tired and will not give in to all those stupid tactics they create. My former manager asked what would it take to get you out of here, I told him to make me his assistant and that would get me out of my office and place me in his. He mumbles something like smart-ass

as he departed; my shift changed suddenly. Now I don't have to look at him!

These women loved the work they performed as much as their families and were willing to endure many barriers to obtain the balance they desired. Although, Participant J expressed her experiences as excessively controlled as she stated:

> It is like being a puppet on a string, you dance when they say dance or you're out. I had to separate from one company because the pressure was immense. Every day it was something else. Do this, why didn't you do that, go here, jump run and always hostile and demanding. I was miserable and I actually liked what I did, just not where I did it. I was so unhappy and stressed it effected my family and home. I had to get out, if only to protect them; Lord knows the pressure was more than I bargained for.

In most cases, the challenges surpassed their desires for balance; prompting many women to leave corporate America to pursue entrepreneurial endeavors or to exit from the realm of business entirely.

The Pittsburgh corporate leadership behavior influencing women is characteristic of differences such as competencies, motives, personality traits, and socio-cultural skills (Ely et al., 2010; Zahidi & Ibarra, 2010). Participants A, C, D, G, H, and J expressed various adverse hurdles, obstacles, and situations encounter within their corporate offices. As Participant D, shared her continually changing and demanding experience as excessive control as she stated:

> It is like being a puppet on a string, you dance when they say dance or you're out. I had to separate form one company because the pressure was immense. Every day it was something else. Do this, why didn't you do that, go here, jump run and always hostile and demanding. Something was always missing, needed or incorrect. I finally got tired and had enough. The only problem is it was exactly what they wanted. On my last day they snickered, and sung, *well, another one bites the dust in the break room.* I cannot begin

to tell you how conflicted I was. I was happy to escape and at the same time wish, I could stay. I was so stressed it effected my family and home. I had to get out, if only to protect them; Lord knows it was much more than I bargained for. I had to admit to my family, and myself I was miserable. I liked what I did, just not where I did it.

Participants C, G, J, and O discussed their best efforts to work within their male-dominated organizations, sometimes is just not enough often leaving them with very limited options beyond exiting the workplace and beginning again. Participant K stated:

I had enough of break room the insults, disrespectful treatment, snide remarks on the elevators and continual battles to prove my self-worth. I thought what the hell am I doing; I am better than this and they know it. I set out to establish my ranking outside of Pittsburgh's corporate arena and (boldly smiling) privately build my empire.

The continual rigidity has prompted many women executives to reconsider their professional paths. Six of the participants engaged in heated office battles to obtain balance. Five participants launched legal actions to obtain congruity on their leadership, role, and 10 had decided to conform to the dynamics of their corporate offices.

As Participant O stated, "I elected to hold off having children so therefore I do not have many issues however, there are something's just not worth fighting. As long as I am adequately paid for, the work I do perform is good enough for me. The only battle I wish to engage in is the battle to retire in peace." Previous research Distelhorst (2005) and recent research conducted by Corea, Guaya, and Lackerb, 2008; Amatucci and Crawley, (2011), proposed these imposed false perceptions have placed women in rigid conflicting positions of rigidity creating turmoil at the home and office. Respondents statements support the problems women in Pittsburgh leadership do encounter obstacles and hurdles because of these imposed gender differences in leadership roles.

Theme 3: Success determinant. Participants A, G, and O discussed differences encountered between men and women maintaining positions with Pittsburg corporate offices. Participant A reflected on expectations for working hours, educational, and proficiencies, requirements women leadership had to achieve to maintain their professional standing or roles of leadership within their predominantly male led organization:

> It was emphatically stated—you are expected to work however long necessary to accomplish your task. This typically means you will be working on an average project approximately 12 hours a day. If this is, an issue for you say so now and spares us replacing you now. The tension was thick and the pressure was on. Do I accept or say never mind. I accepted and every conceivable challenged was hurled my way and had me thinking I should have said NO!

Women in the Pittsburgh corporate arena are placed or accept the most difficult positions continually present professional acuity however continue to encounter gender bias and unfair obstacles in ascent to leadership.

According to Eagly and Carli (2007), women viewed as successful in leadership was abnormally rare by their male colleagues. Though women continually demonstrate their leadership acuity gender biases continue to present hindrances of advancement and success. Participant E professed:

> We have some strong women leaders in my organization who are causally viewed and continually dismissed. Let's face it women could come up with an amazing protocol and it would not be readily accepted without being sanctioned by some male leader who would attach his claim to the process.

The reality of these gendered biased perceptions result in behaviors, classification, and cultural traits typically associated by gender (Al-Lamky & Aysa, 2007). These perceptions possess different attitudes, physical attributes, and reactions that create an unfair determination of qualifications for women leadership in the Pittsburg corporate arena.

Early research (Distelhorst, 2005), pointed to many women capable ready to assume upper leadership roles as more recent studies (Corea, Guaya, & Lackerb, 2008; Amatucci & Crawley,

2011) concurred, however gender biases created ever-changing barriers preventing the ascent into roles of upper-level leadership within the Pittsburgh corporate arena. Of the two hundred forty-six pages of transcribed interviews, seventy-five percent of the participants expressed a notable difference that remains a male dominant perception that women are incapable of leadership and therefore should not lead men; further promoting and sustaining the struggle for women in this area. Participant D expressed:

> Men believe women cannot lead men, they can only lead women, in general gender biases and assumptions in my office is ever present, whether we acknowledge it or not. That assumption is that women could not and should not lead or should not be leaders at any level that extends power or authority over their male colleagues.

The reality of gender bias for the respondents in Pittsburgh, Pennsylvania corporate arena today is that it remains an ongoing battle within the corporate arena (Catalyst, 2007; (Corea, Guaya, & Lackerb, 2008; Amatucci & Crawley, 2011). Participant F recalled the difficulties encountered as she assumed the lead position on a project:

> The project was simple, the assignments were given, however the men in the division rejected my approach, and refused to follow direction. Their refusal led to the hot seat because certain tasks were incomplete. I had to replace the staff to get the project done. Yes, I replaced each one with a woman.

The discord between men and women is a result of encroachment and entitlement. Women will never be welcomed as long as men feel women have invaded their territory. "There is an unspoken expectation of entitlement that a woman should never lead men" (Participant B). This remains a considerable barrier in the Pittsburgh corporate offices. The supposition is, as women continue to make cultural changes in abilities, education, career ambitions, job preferences, personalities, and workplace participations increases, organizations, and culture may change (Eagly & Carli, 2007)

In the Pittsburgh corporate arena women remain outnumbered from entry-level to upper-level leadership roles with few opportunities of advancement. Previous research considered gender bias as the norms and practices of male-dominated organizations (Distelhorst, 2005), in conjunction with recent studies, (Eagly et al., 2007; Corea, Guaya, & Lackerb, 2008; Amatucci & Crawley, 2011), concur. A small number of women have reached the upper levels of leadership in their organization; seldom has the number of women in upper level leadership exceeded 5% (Catalyst, 2011b).

The number of women in upper level leadership roles examined in these investigation-included women in Pittsburgh's, corporate arena in those roles did not have the power and influence of their male colleagues. In some case, the titles, and roles listed were the same however; the responsibilities and visible exposures were not. These women held positions behind the scenes, provided easy implementation, and exacted minimal power and authority beyond the scope of their office. Participant E stated, "the position I currently hold is identical in title however, salary and responsibilities are another issue entirely."

Women with demonstrated records of accomplishment of success continue to encounter gender barriers as they ascend or attempt to ascend the corporate ladder. In the Pittsburgh corporate arena, despite recognized successful leadership women have to fight for the same titles of leadership readily given to their male colleagues (Haney, 2010). Participant C recalled a long battle for the role as vice president. Her accomplishments and responsibilities out shadowed her male colleagues, yet she was denied. Participant G:

> My responsibilities were excessive and included regularly managing million dollar accounts. Whereas my male colleagues' accounts never exceeded $500,000 in net worth, yet they were elevated to vice president. The reassignment and designation of the position was the outcome of the long-term battle for me. It was also a realization of the extent I could go.

Participant O aptly summarized the gender bias subtheme as follows: "Men are promoted on potential, and sometimes, women are promoted on their records of accomplishments. Just don't hold your breath waiting for a promotion."

Theme 4: Emotions. The emotional segregation discussed in this research coincides with previous studies (Eagly & Sczesny, 2009; Euwema et al., 2007) about issues of isolation encountered by women in culturally male-dominated leadership roles. The segregation encountered, diminished passion, and continual battle for equality often led to women separating from their organizations (Davis et al., 2010). In this investigative approach, 12 of participants liked their positions and 4 expressed some degree of empowerment in their leadership roles. Women entering the Pittsburgh corporate arena have increased forging new levels of networking outside their organizations; forming associations of support similar to the male dominant associations to aid women's ascent to upper-level leadership. The emerging subthemes associated to the emotion theme are loneliness and stress.

Subtheme: Loneliness. Eight of 15 participants expressed a degree of loneliness experienced in their pursuit for upper-level leadership roles. Also noted in their responses is the lack of female support or mentorship (Eagly & Carli, 2007). In the midst of a pressured filled, gender bias environment women executives encounter and battle loneliness. This loneliness stems from both male and female presence in the organization (Euwema et al., 2007). Women who assume upper leadership roles segregate themselves from the workforce to prove worthiness and empowerment. Participant F declared

> As the VP I had a leadership what was constantly under fire. I got grief from every area of the workplace. If I appeared laidback with my staff, my leadership came into question. If I led in a rigid process, my staff was not happy. I soon found myself all alone in a workplace that had over 100 members.

Women experiences within the workplace often result in loneliness because of lack of support that their male colleagues have. In the Pittsburgh arena, male leadership finds readily fellowship with other male colleagues, support organizations, resources, and tools not readily available to women (Distelhorst, 2005). Seven of the participants acknowledged the limitation of resources provided to support their leadership roles. Further indicated by Participant G, "if we (women) truly want to be in the know we have to learn to empower ourselves and build resources related to our approaches and acuities."

   Subtheme: Stress. Thirteen of participants expressed concern about the degree of stress associated to their executive pursuits. The stress encountered by women leaders stemmed from various aspects within their corporations. These aspects extended from competition to gender and sexism discriminations (Davis et al., 2010). Each participant discussed a form of stress-related experiences associated to what Participant B referred to as "the good old boy network" that has a sole purpose to undermine or block any level of corporate advancement, stating, "at one point the president said he will never see a proper fit for women in leadership. They are emotional amoebae's totally out of their league and lack the ability to lead anything beyond the home." Because of the level of stress, a number of the participants have elected to separate from their corporate arenas to start their own companies. Those participants who have also indicated stressors associated to their endeavors. However, these stressors are appropriate presenting a different set of challenges for women leaders. Participant O exuberantly stated:

> I love the challenges I face now. The stress level is probably equal to what I endured at that corporation. However, this is my company and my single objective to please anyone is me! I love the competition at this level and know with each battle I win, I WIN!.

Additionally participants expressed a small hope that there will be balance someday within their corporate offices.

   Theme 5: Leadership roles. Women leadership roles are often conflicted, disapproved and experience significant biases with every effort to ascend the corporate ladder (Heilman, & Eagly, 2008). As women assume culturally male dominate roles of leadership in Pittsburgh Pennsylvania, many have assume these roles and demonstrate the same gender biases upon their workforces. These biases include asserted masculine deportment, rigidity and what Participant B called "a Commando Atmosphere," boldly declaring:

> I do not see the problem being the only female at this level. I grew up in a male dominant environment and have no issues with it at all. They [her male colleagues] know I can handle myself and my workforce knows my expectations of them. I get results or I get replacements. I am in control either way!

Theme 6: Labyrinthine phenomenon. A labyrinth begins to form as women strategically maneuver between continuing discrimination, family responsibilities, and stereotypical bias. As women seek to ascend the corporate ladder, they encounter hurdles that result in a difference in perception and treatment in Pittsburgh's corporate arena. Eagly and Carli (2007) contended some women successfully maneuver these obstacles and find their way through the labyrinth and reach upper executive offices. Most (85%) of the participant expressed the many hurdles and perceptions of their abilities in relationship to this labyrinthine phenomenon. Participant A:

> After working for five years in a sublevel position it became apparent to advance, I needed to have the skills and knowledge to do so. I took a Hiatus for four years. I had two children and I graduated with honors with an MBA. When I sought employment with my former employer; I was summarily rejected. Reason given, the responsibilities were rigid, requiring an individual who could sustain the pace and requirements. You do not fit that description, obviously having other responsibilities that would distract or hammer your work.

Responses such as this support the premise that the labyrinthine phenomenon has become the new glass ceiling for women the Pittsburgh corporate arena.

Eight participants expounded on other aspects of the labyrinthine phenomenon that imposed hindrance or completely blocked their efforts to ascend the corporate ladder.

Participants A, and G in two different environments expressed occurrences of the labyrinth as Participant A stated

I worked hard to gain the credentials I have. There was not a problem with my leadership until I returned from maternity leave and suddenly I could not perform adequately enough. My position was no longer available and I was demoted (of course they did not see it that way); from a mid-level executive management position to an administrative directors position. My staff now consisted of a small pool of administrative assistance, AKA secretaries.

Participant G stated:

My mother had a medical situation that required immediate care. Forced to take time away from the office to establish the necessary requirements; I returned to the workplace and was suddenly not welcomed. When I departed, I was assured my duties would be here when I return. Not the case, the organization sited a need to move forward and with that move, a revision of responsibilities was established. According to the newly formed assignment, I was no longer fit. I was welcomed back in another division under the leadership of a male who had less experience them me. My prior accomplishments no longer mattered the only thing management focused on was the probable need to tend to family needs again.

Participant after participant reflected upon some form of bias associated with the labyrinthine phenomenon.

Findings: Research and Questions

Research of this investigative approach included two research questions. The research questions were the following: What barriers do women in Pittsburgh, Pennsylvania, corporate arena perceive as inhibiting their promotion in the workplace? What are the reasons women are leaving Pittsburgh, Pennsylvania, corporate offices, and abandoning the pursuit of executive leadership roles? The six emerging themes in this discussion identified treatment by corporation, success determinants, leadership roles, labyrinthine phenomenon, emotions, and challenges. Five subthemes were identified family obligations, gender bias, stress, emotional discord, loneliness, and the labyrinth phenomenon.

Finding from the themes identified characteristics of gender bias (a) dismissive behavior toward women in leadership roles, (b) unwarranted leadership roles, (c) double standards of family obligation, and (d) refusal to integrate the work-life leadership models.

A characteristic of gender bias was dismissive behavior toward women holding culturally male-dominated leadership roles. Participant H stated, "I have attained one of the highest offices in the organizations and during a board meeting was asked to go get coffee!" Participant M discussed an assignment to take on a vacant position. When she said was not interested unless the position was going to be hers. Management agreed, and she filled that position for one year:

> I arrived to the office to find the director and chairman in my office along with an unknown male. Informing me the unknown male was the new head of the department a position I had held for the past year, in addition, I was to get him acclimated to the position. No discussion, or heads up.

Lack of empowerment is another characteristic of gender bias. Women holding typically male-oriented positions roles had token positions with little or no power. These positions serve as window dressing and law appeasement for organizations. Participant C stated:

> I was given a position as Director and Lead administrator. In print, it looks impressive. In reality, it is nothing more than window dressing. My title is toss around as some banner of success, when in reality. I am in charge of the secretary pool and temporary staff. Far from the original description but why rock the boat, I'm a short termer and happy to have missed the last two cutbacks.

In addition are the double standards of gender women in leadership encounter. These are indicative to women who attend to family needs, obligations, or seek to enhance expertise. Social role theory focuses on the double standards of men and women. The societal assumption is that women are caregivers, responsible home, and children. These double standards therefore become submergence as characteristic associated to male organizational leadership expectations, and roles (Heilman & Eagly, 2008). Participant E stated, "I really do not care how they feel, my family comes first. If that means I have to struggle more or endure their crap, so be it." However, Participant O declared does not apply to me, no children, and no family obligation to distract."

A final characteristic of gender bias double standards associated to assignments and tasks performed by women. These were often assignments or tasks no one else would assume. Tasks that required lengthy hours, massive grunt work and zero benefits. Women in assumed these roles as proof of their acumen and performance abilities (Henry-Brown & Campbell-Lewis, 2005). Participant stated:

> I sought many noteworthy positions well within the scope of my abilities and was denied every time. Then a position surface that had many issues and not one male had applied. I sought the job thinking if I pull this off they will have to recognize my skills.

The resulting perception of the participants revealed double standards indicative of a lack of respect and flexibility for women in leadership roles. A double standard applied to women in leadership who pursued education that enhanced expertise. The over arcing double standard begins as women are informed that they lack abilities for an upper-level positions. As women seek to fulfill these requirements, a double standard emerges, penalizing women for taking time away from work while their male colleagues are not (Henry-Brown & Campbell-Lewis, 2005). Participant B stated:

> I literally watched them push a coworker (female) out the door after she took time off to obtain a Masters–MBA. If we (women) learned anything from that, it is to find a way to get educated and work at the same time. That's not doable for everyone, but truly wise.

Another result revealed perception of inabilities associated with gender bias and family obligations. Organizational perception of a culturally male-dominated arena reveals a double standard apply to women not realized by their male colleagues. The double standards create evolving obstacles and completely block advancement (Eagly & Carli, 2007; Henry-Brown & Campbell-Lewis, 2005). Participant A stated:

> I was interviewing for a position, responding the standard questions when all of a sudden he said; 'You have two kids, right. How is that helpful to your role?' I was totally taken aback by this. I said my, kids are my life! The interview ended and the position went to a man.

A final aspect of gender bias identified in participant responses was the refusal to integrate a work-life model of leadership into the corporate arena (McCrimmon, 2012). Historically have women struggled with leadership as defined by a culturally male dominant perspective. Consider women who demonstrate an inclusive behavior are deficient and incapable of leadership (Davis et al., 2010; Eagly & Carli, 2007). Perceptions such as these are continuing hindrances for women pursuing leadership roles in Pittsburgh's corporate arena.

As the global corporate arena advances, innovation, and new corporate structures emerge new approaches to leadership and leadership theories surface such as Theory U (Scharmer, 2009). Theory U is used to guide organizations and leadership through different approaches to structural development, workforce interaction, strategy implementation, and workplace dynamics. According to Scharmer (2009), Theory U offers both a new theoretical perspective and a practical social technology. As a theoretical perspective, Theory U suggests that the way in which we attend to a situation determines how a situation unfolds: I attend this way, therefore it emerges that way. As a practical social technology, Theory U offers a set of principles and practices for collectively creating the future that wants to emerge (following the movements of co-initiating, co-sensing, co-inspiring, co-creating, and co-evolving) (Presencing Institute, 2012).

R1. What barriers do women in the Pittsburgh, Pennsylvania, corporate arena perceive as inhibiting their promotion in the workplace? Many participants discussed discrimination, heightened hostilities, and issues of isolation, extreme job demands, gender bias, and lack of support encountered in their pursuit to ascend the corporate ladder. These barriers exact an enormous degree of pressure that not realized by their male colleagues. Because of the incessant uneven unbalanced barriers and pressures, women are reconsidering their options to stay in the leadership race or withdraw entirely (Davis et al., 2010; Eagly & Carli, 2007).

The extent of the barrier and the extent of their goal to ascend the corporate ladder; women are seeking strategies for success. Various participants indicated an acceptance of lengthy work hours, personal sacrifices, and enhancing knowledge and skill sets is necessary if they are to succeed (Davis et al., 2010). "I believe we (women), have to buck up, nobody likes it when I say this but it's real. If I truly want this I must jump in and do what is necessary to succeed" (Participant K).

Eight out of 15 participants discussed the hardships endured by the barriers they encounter are established to take away our pride and dignity. "In my company it is common to hear men whisper some insult or degrading comment. In some cases, the discrimination is blatant, especially if we react or respond. The barrier of discrimination is the most difficult for me" (Participant H). Recognizing the extent of these barriers has prompted new approaches by women as they ascend the corporate ladder.

R2. What are the reasons women are leaving corporate offices in the Pittsburgh, Pennsylvania, and abandoning the pursuit of executive leadership roles? Six of 15 participants forfeited family interaction for forced and lengthy office hours, lost retrievable family moments to ascend or sustain leadership roles. Four participants revealed how their pursuits in the corporate arena affect their current or previous marriages. No matter the effort or sacrifice, women continue to excel at a slower pace than their male colleagues do (Eagly & Carli, 2007; Corea, Guaya, & Lackerb, 2008; Amatucci & Crawley, 2011).

The extents of the hindrances and challenges women encounter that gender bias imposes have women considering their efforts to attain leadership. Because of heightened hostilities, issues of isolation, extreme job demands, and lack of support women are considering their options to stay in the race or withdraw entirely

(Davis et al., 2010; Eagly & Carli, 2007). "I looked at the weight of the strain I placed on my family to achieve my goals and have to ask, is it worth it" (Participant G). Respondents discussed numerous accounts of frustration that led to their colleagues leaving the corporate arena (Eagly et al, 2007 & 2009; Catalyst 2010; Corea, Guaya, & Lackerb, 2008; Amatucci & Crawley, 2011). Participants G and J associated the separation to the depth of issues and hindrances imposed upon women in the Pittsburgh, Pennsylvania arena.

Participant J conveyed her disappointment as follows:

There is nothing worse than enduring daily battles to prove our self-worth. We're competent and capable and ultimately the strong hold on while other retreat. I have not reached a point of retreat yet. It is hard, I understand why those women have left, and for those of us who stay, we're fighting for us all.

Women are continually hindered by the lack of opportunities to advance; encounter unequal organizational dynamics, and discrimination, women executives leave larger organizations pursuing entrepreneurial endeavors (Eagly et al., 2007; Haney, 2010; (Corea, Guaya, & Lackerb, 2008; Amatucci & Crawley, 2011). Participant O said:

It's not the barriers inasmuch as it is the ever changing twist and turns of the leadership journey. Hell, the glass ceiling is forever, and expected it is the new way they prevent our success by instituting obstacles that force us to go down paths men do not have to travel to succeed.

Summary of Findings

Obstacles and barriers created by gender bias continue to impede the advancement of women seeking upper-level leadership roles in the Pittsburgh, Pennsylvania's, corporate arena. The appearances of gender biases included contemptuous behavior, unwarranted leadership roles, double standards of family responsibility, absence of mentor and leadership support, a failure to integrate work-life balances, and failed implementation of women leadership roles. Because of the continual encounters with gender, bias women are reconsidering their approach to ascend the corporate ladder and exploring options of separating from corporate America entirely to initiate their own companies.

Implications of Important Findings

The intent of this investigation was to explore the lived experiences of women who occupied culturally male-dominated leadership roles. Six main themes and five subtheme emerged from this investigation suggested the effects of gender bias diminished the talent and expertise available to organizations. As previously discussed within the emergent themes the continuing impact of gender bias women in culturally male dominant leadership roles is treasonous, and continues to undermine and discourage the success of women in the Pittsburgh corporate arena.

The perception is women in the Pittsburgh corporate arena are under qualified for leadership. Women, though many women have demonstrated records of accomplishment are also considered not qualified for leadership roles that require management over males. Participant D held several powerless positions given as appeasement to demands to promote more women into upper management roles. Participants G, K, M, and O experienced disadvantages because of the perceptions that women lacked the proficiency to perform and were view as inadequate in comparison to their male colleagues. Shared disadvantages were women lack the ability to perform in leadership roles as proficiently as men were and women represented a level of inequality in comparison to their male colleagues.

Whether women abandon or are excluded from upper leaders a significant void is present the Pittsburgh corporate arena. Acceptance of acts of biasness gender specific or otherwise does not promote an inclusive workforce or working environment (Duehr & Bono, 2006). A collaborative and inclusive workplace environment is the organization of the future (Scharmer, 2009). Global changes to organizational structures recognize the deficiency associated to having a conflicted environment not is an inclusive and supportive of the entire working environment. How women are received, viewed, and promotionally advanced may become a detriment to organizations unwilling to implement changes for the perceptions of how women, change (Yukl, 2010). Globally, leadership is highly dependent on building relationships between leaders and followers both men and women.

According to Yukl (2010), the leader should try to establish a special exchange relationship with all subordinates if possible, not just with a few favorites. Yukl (2010) associated a dyadic relationship in terms of the leader-member exchange (LMX), which is the relationship building between a leader and each individual subordinate and the exchange relationship that develops over time. Additionally, a leader's position or upward mobility is another important determining factor of the potential for establishing a favorable exchange relationship with subordinates (Yukl, 2010). If a workforce not feel like the leader is well respected in the organization, he or she may be reluctant to develop a strong bond with the leader; furthermore, how followers view leader competence and intentions have implications for leadership effectiveness (Wolfram, Mohr, & Schyns, 2006; Yukl, 2010).

The focus of this investigation is Pittsburgh, Pennsylvania's, corporate arena to develop knowledge associated to the scope of labyrinthine phenomenon generated by gender biases what are lived by women seeking upper-level leadership roles. The number of women in corporate offices has increased in spite continuing issues related to the glass ceiling. However, the labyrinthine phenomenon significantly hinders the advancement of women today as they encounter a maze of obstacles generated by male constructs and biases of leadership. Women have moved beyond the in-house training sessions obtaining graduate and postgraduate degrees and still battle perceptions of inadequacy from their peers. Many women have abandoned their pursuits of leadership in the corporate realm to start businesses of their own and still report issues of qualification from their peers.

Recommendations for Leadership

Based on the emergent themes of this investigation the following suggested recommendations developed because of the knowledge, and actual experiences discussed in this investigation. The recommendations are to assist women seeking to ascend the corporate ladder in a male-dominated arena. The first recommendation is to develop an equivalent right of entry protocols non-gender specific. The second establish work life protocols to establish balance in the workplace. The third recommendation is to establish inclusive networking initiatives. The fourth recommendation is Establish Work Life balance. The fifth recommendation is to establish company-wide communication systems.

Equivalent right of entry protocol. Current trends in male-dominated organization impede or hinder advancement for women. Establishing nonspecific and non-gendered processes of advancement would eliminate eventually decreased the presence of women in upper level leadership roles. Organizations can accomplish this by making opportunities of advancement available company-wide and using a blind selection process that would eliminate gender entirely from consideration. The development of equivalent right of entry protocols would process advancement to upper-level leadership roles solely on acumen and not gender.

Establish work life protocols to establish balance in the work-place. Work-life issues are mounting daily in the corporate arena. However, if women are nurturers and family obligations is their forte penalizing women when attending to those needs is inappropriate (Eagly & Carli, 2007). Organizations have to take one a greater sense of responsibility for family obligations. The implementation of processes that support the work forces needs when family obligations occur would only serve to benefit the organization. These protocols would establish processes for time off with assurance of job stability and permanency. Corporations exacting these protocols would also witness a decrease in stress and emotional discord company-wide moreover within the ranks of women seeking to ascend the corporate ladder. .

Establish inclusive networking initiatives. The global view of organizations today frowns upon organizations that have not or refuse to be inclusive. Establishing networking initiatives inclusive will promote collaboration, decrease turnover, heighten productivity, and create higher morale within the work-place. Another advantage of implementing inclusive initiatives increases organizational flexibility and learned knowledge throughout the work-place. As organizations, improve approaches of how they interact with their workforces the organization will witness a decrease in exposure to legal actions and greater recruitment and retention. Other business-related reasons to become more inclusive include the potential to tap into new donor pools, improve program delivery, and reach out to new clients or audiences (Cox, 2012).

Establish work life balance. Today's organization must move forward to create a balanced work-place that includes initiatives that address the issue of work-life balance. The issue of work-life balance is becoming more important to workforces company-wide. The need for organizations to establish work-life balance will continue as diversity (age, cultural, ethnic, etc.) in the workplace increases and as technology and social media promotes connectivity (Cohen, 2011). Corporations, implementing of work-life balance initiatives biases of every magnitude could eliminate at the corporate arena.

Establish Initiatives for retention. The overall perception conveyed in the investigation indicated disconnection, and lack of collaboration, or cohesive partnership, in the corporate arena. Because of this perception, women have positioned themselves and assumed to one of three postures. 1) They resigned themselves to the notion of closure, denied access, and advancement limitation, 2) Resistance to the notions of inabilities and fight for advancement regardless of the struggle or hostility, or 3) Abandonment; many women abandoned their pursuit to upper level leadership as a result of the overwhelming pressure.

Women in the Pittsburgh, Pennsylvania corporate offices would benefit from initiatives to retain professional women. As many of the respondent conveyed, (Participant, A, B, C, D, E, F, H, I, J, and L) the need for challenge is always welcomed in business however, unwarranted constraints and obstacles that prevent advancement at any level is not productive. The battle continues to present a monumental challenge for women it in the Pittsburgh Pennsylvania corporate arena. The labyrinth phenomenon has become an enormous issue for women in Pittsburgh, Pennsylvania. Once a women steps out of the corporate office to handle life events of any proportion, returning to the workforce is met with unrealistic twisting challenges, obstacles and barriers. These continued hostile actions infringed on women have invoked valid considerations to remain in the corporate office or to leave to explore other business or entrepreneurial endeavors.

According to these participants, those who have explored those options outside of the corporate arena, find the pressures to succeed far more rewarding. Women in Pittsburgh are finding rewards and accomplishments outside the arena that were not possible within the corporate arena in spite of how they are judged or viewed a male-dominated society.

If the Pittsburgh, Pennsylvania corporate arena initiates protocols and procedures, focusing on the return and reinstatement of women to the corporate office a collaborative environment could be realized. Women would reconsider abandoning their executive pursuits, the corporate arena would benefit from a vast array of talent and possibilities of growth.

Establish company-wide communication systems. It was apparent throughout the investigation that communications was a major flaw in the corporate arena. The need to have a process of communications companywide if paramount and can no longer be one-sided. Information is vital to the success of every organization. When communications break down information ceases to flow, workforces become disoriented, disillusioned, and intimidated. Today's organizations need to establish communications knowledge and proficiencies to promote understanding and bridge communication gaps companywide. This would mean that upper-level leaders no hold company knowledge within their ranks but share company information and processes top-down and bottom-up (Hesselbein & Goldsmith, 2006; Cashman, 2008).

Generalization to other population. Consideration to the generalization to other population in this qualitative investigative approach provides opportunity for future investigation and examination of the effects of labyrinth theory. The investigation designed could be associated the collection, and analysis of different data sources from a qualitative method that provides an in-depth perspective of the additional populations in Pittsburgh Pennsylvania's corporate arena (McQueen et al., 2006; Neuman, 2007; Leedy & Ormrod, 2010). The population would be applicable to (a) aspiring young women 25-35 seeking advance to leadership positions; (b) older women 55-65 with tenure in leadership roles, (c) leaders who mentor other women advancement to leadership positions; and (d), all men and women seeking opportunities of advancement to leadership positions.

Recommendation for Future Research

In review of data collected, the following recommendations for future research emerge. Future studies could focus on the navigating the effects (barriers, mazes, and obstacles) labyrinthine phenomenon, perceptions of gender bias in relationship to the labyrinthine phenomenon, leadership analysis, and perceived leadership acumen of men and women. The first recommendation would be to expand the scope of participants to include men. An inclusion of men would broaden comprehension of perceived gender biases, perspective of male-dominated work environments, perceptions of the treatment of women in corporate America. A second recommendation conduct a qualitative leadership analysis on the impact of emotional stressors derived from various forms of gender bias in the workplace. A third recommendation an investigation comparing the perceived versus real lived experiences of male-dominate leadership for both men and women. A fourth recommendation, to conduct an examination on comparable qualifications possessed by men and required by women as requirement for advancement to upper-level leadership roles. A fifth recommendation, to investigate the effects of networking using mentoring building versus the absence of networking and mentoring for women in male dominant work environments.

Summary

The exploration of this investigation was to gain comprehension of the experiences of women in leadership in culturally male-dominated environments within the Pittsburgh corporate offices. The theoretical framework for this investigative approach was the theory of the labyrinth phenomenon. Previous research (Eagly, 1987; Eagly & Carli, 2007), indicated that the concept of women in leadership in male dominate organizations creates conflict, exhibits gender bias, barriers, and obstacles. According to 12 of the participants shared their experiences of navigating unwarranted maze like obstacles in their attempts to maintain current leadership roles or ascend to upper-level leadership roles the Pittsburgh corporate arena. These unwarranted actions prompted women to reconsider their pursuits to attain upper level leaderships or abandon their pursuits entirely and launch their own businesses.

Women are finding ways to navigate the labyrinthine maze of obstacles. Further research of the labyrinth phenomenon may enable organizations to make the structural changes necessary to diminish the gender bias maze of obstacles and hurdles women must overcome to advance in leadership. Six main themes emerged treatment by industry standards, challenges, success determinants, emotions, leadership roles, and the labyrinthine phenomenon. Five subthemes were identified family obligations, gender bias, stress, loneliness, and the labyrinth phenomenon. Finding from the themes identified characteristics of gender bias, dismissive behavior toward women in leadership roles, precarious leadership roles, double standards of family obligation, and refusal to integrate the work-life leadership models. It was evident from the labyrinthine investigation that gender bias continues to present major barrier for women in Pittsburgh leadership. The obstacles demonstrated by gender bias included discrimination, dismissive behavior, a double standard that exhibited unwarranted obstacles, and unrealistic expectations imposed on women only. In addition, Pittsburgh corporate offices fail to integrate work life balance, and leadership models for women.

As long as corporations continue to exclude women from the ranks of upper-level, leadership organizations will not realize the depth of talent and expertise available. Furthermore, the continuation of hostile treatment and implementation of unwarranted obstacles will drive more women out of the corporate arena and into entrepreneurial endeavors. A recommendation of the continue research into the effects of labyrinthine phenomenon on women in leadership.

References

Avolio, B. J., & Yammarino, F. J. (Eds.) (2008). *Transformational and charismatic leadership: The road ahead.* Bingley, England: Emerald.

Barreto, M., Ryan, M. K., & Schmitt, M. T. (2009). Introduction: Is the glass ceiling still relevant in the 21st century? In M. Barreto, M. K. Ryan, M. T. Schmitt, M. Barreto, M. K. Ryan, M. T. Schmitt (Eds.), *The glass ceiling in the 21st century: Understanding barriers to gender equality* (pp. 3–18). Washington, DC: American Psychological Association. doi:10.1037/11863-001

Barusch, A., Gringeri, C., & George, M. (2011). Rigor in qualitative social work research: A Review of strategies used in published articles. *Social Work Research, 35*(1), 11–19.

Bendl, R., & Schmidt, A. (2010). From "glass ceilings" to "firewalls"—different metaphors for describing discrimination. *Gender, Work & Organization, 17*(5), 612–634. doi:10.1111/j.1468-0432.2010.00520.x

Bennis, W. (2009). Leadership advantage: Leader to leader. Retrieved from http://www.hr newcorp.com/articles/bennis_Leaders.pdf

Berry, P., & Franks, T. J. (2010). Women in the world of corporate business: Looking at the glass ceiling. *Contemporary Issues in Education Research, 3*(2), 1–9.

Biddle, B., & Thomas, E. (1979.) *Role theory: Concepts and research.* Huntington, NY: Kreige.

Brown, K. R. (1999). *Divided labours: An evolutionary view of women at work.* New Haven, CT: Yale University.

Business Women First. (2011-2012). Business women first. The Business Journals. Retrieved from http://www.bizjournals.com/

Capretta, C., Clark, L. P., & Guangrong, D. (2008). Executive derailment: Three cases in point and how to prevent it.

Global Business & Organizational Excellence, 27(3), 48-56. doi:10.1002/joe.20203Cashman, K. (2008). Leadership from the inside out: Becoming a leader for life (2nd ed.). San Francisco, CA: Berrett-Koehler.

Catalyst. (2008). Catalyst census of women in corporate offices and top earners of the Fortune 500. Retrieved from: http://www.catalyst.org/publication/238/2008-catalyst-census-of-women-corporate-offices-and-top-earners-of-the-fortune-500

Catalyst. (2011a). African-American women. Retrieved from http://www.catalyst.org/publication/222/african-american-women

Catalyst. (2011b). Catalyst census of women in U.S. management. Retrieved from http://www.catalyst.org/publication/206/women-in-us-management

Catalyst. (2011c). Statistical overview of women in the workplace. New York: Catalyst. Retrieved from http://www.catalyst.org/publication/219/statistical-overview-of-women-in-the-workplace

Catalyst. (2011d). U.S. women in business. Retrieved from http://www.catalyst.org/publication/132/us-women-in-business

Cohen, J. (2011). Work-life balance: 7 keys to work life balance. Retrieved from http://www.7keystoworklifebalance.com/about/

Connelly, S., & Ruark, G. (2010). Leadership style and activating potential moderators of the

relationships among leader emotional displays and outcomes. The Leadership Quarterly, 21(5), 745-764. Elsevier Inc. Retrieved from http://linkinghub.elsevier.com/retrieve/pii/S104898431000012 19

Cox, T. (2012). Developing competency to manage diversity, San Francisco, CA: Berrett-Koehler.

Davis, M., Capobianco, S., & Kraus, L. (2010). Gender differences in responding to conflict in the workplace: Evidence from a large sample of working adults. *Sex Roles, 63*(7/8), 500–514. doi:10.1007/s11199-010-9828-9

Distelhorst, D. J. (2005). Dominance and deference: Status expectations of men and women. *Diversity Factor, 13*(2), 24.

Duehr, E. E., & Bono, J. E. (2006). Men, women, and managers: Are stereotypes finally changing? *Personnel Psychology, 59*(4), 815–846. doi:10.1111/j.1744-6570.2006 .00055.x

Eagly, A. H, (1987). *Sex differences in social behavior: A social-role interpretation.* Hillsdale, NJ: Erlbaum.

Eagly, A. H., & Carli, L. L. (2007). *Through the labyrinth: The truth about how women become leaders.* Boston, MA: Harvard Business School Press.

Eagly, A. H., & Sczesny, S. (2009). Stereotypes about women, men, and leaders: Have times changed? In M. Barreto, M. K. Ryan, & M. T. Schmitt (Eds.), *The glass ceiling in the 21st century: Understanding barriers to gender equality* (pp. 21–47). Washington, DC: American Psychological Association. doi:10.1037/11863 -002

Ely, R. J., Ibaarrs, H., & Kolb, D. M. (2011). Taking gender into account: Theory and design for women's leadership development programs. *Academy of Management Learning and Education, 10*(3), 474–493.

Euwema, M., Wendt, H., & Van Emmerik, H. (2007). Leadership styles and group

Fade, S. (2004). Using interpretative phenomenological analysis for public health nutrition and dietetic research: a practical guide. Proceedings of the Nutrition Society (63) pp. 647–653. DOI:10.1079/PNS2004398

Grassi, E. (2009). What is existential-phenomenology? Heidegger and Renaissance Humanism, pp. 90-9. Retrieved from http://www.mythosandlogos.com/whatep.html

Greenwald, J. (2006). Women make strides in industry, but still face challenges. *Business Insurance, 40*(41), 12–14.

Grout, P. A., Park, I-U., & Sonderegger, S. (2007). *An economic theory of the glass ceiling.* Retrieved from http://www.bris.ac.uk/depts./CMPO/working paper/wp183pdf

Güngör, G., & Biernat, M. (2009). Gender bias or motherhood disadvantage? Judgments of blue collar mothers and fathers in the workplace. *Sex Roles*, 60(3/4), 232–246. doi:10.1007/s11199-008-9540-1

Haney, W. G. (2010). Successes visible, but obstacles remain: Women managers and entrepreneurs in today's workplaces. *Feminist Collections: A Quarterly of Women's Studies Resources, 31*(4), 1–6.

Hansen, S. (2009). Cracks in the glass ceiling? *Sex roles, 60*(9/10), 748–750. doi:10.1007/s11199-008-9546-8.

Heilman, M. E., & Eagly, A. H. (2008). Gender stereotypes are alive, well, and busy producing workplace discrimination. *Industrial and Organizational Psychology, 1*(4), 393–398. doi:10.1111/j.1754-9434.2008.00072.x

Henry, M. (2009). Overcome the 3 reasons leaders fail to reflect on the past. Retrieved from http://leadchangegroup.com/overcome-3-reasons-leaders-fail-reflect/

Henry-Brown, R., & Campbell-Lewis, N. (2005). Examining barriers to career advancement among females of color in the federal career service. *Race, Gender, and Class, 12*(3/4), 31–47.

Hesselbein, F., & Goldsmith, M. (Eds.). (2006). *The leader of the future 2: Visions, strategies, and practices for the new era.* San Francisco, CA: Jossey-Bass.

Hester, R. (2007). The glass ceiling and its effect on women. Retrieved from http://www.associatedcontent.com/article/248276/the glass ceiling and its effect on.html

Hewlett, S. A. 2007. *Off ramps and on ramps: Keeping talented women on the road to success.* Boston, MA: Harvard Business School Press.

Hinton, K. G. (2006). The true meaning of mentorship. *Diverse Issues in Higher Education, 23*(20), 60–61.

Hogue, M. (2010). The relevance of the glass ceiling for women today. *Psychology of Women Quarterly, 34*(2), 265–266. doi:10.1111/j.1471-6402.2010.01568.x

Hoogland, R. C. (2007). Gender theories. In F. Malti-Douglas (Ed.), *Encyclopedia of sex and gender* (Vol. 2, pp. 628–632). Detroit, MI: Macmillan.

Hopkins, M. M., O'Neil, D.A., & Bilimoria, D. (2006). Effective leadership and successful career advancement: Perspectives from women in health care. *Equal Opportunities International, 25*(4) 251.

Houghton, C., Casey, D., Shaw, D., & Murphy, K. (2010). Ethical challenges in qualitative research: Examples from practice. *Nurse Researcher, 18*(1), 15–25.

House, R. J., Hanges, P. J., Javidan, M., Dorfman, P. W, & Gupta, V. (2004). *Culture, leadership, and organizations. The GLOBE study of 62 societies.* London, England: Sage.

Hymowitz, C., & Schellhardt, T. (1986, March 24). The glass ceiling: Why women can't seem to break the invisible barrier that blocks them from the top jobs. *The Wall Street Journal, 3*(24), 225.

Kessler-Harris, A. (2004). Women's history in the new millennium. *Journal of Women's History, 15*(4), 186–206.

Koenig, A. M., Eagly, A. H., Mitchell, A. A., & Ristikari, T. (2011). Are leader stereotypes masculine? A meta-analysis of three research paradigms. *Psychological Bulletin, 137*(4), 616–642. doi:10.1037/a0023557

Kouzes, J. M., & Posner, B. Z. (2002). *Leadership: The challenge* (4th ed.). San Francisco, CA: Jossey-Bass.

Kreuger, L. W., & Neuman, W. L. (2006). S*ocial work research methods with research navigator.* Upper Saddle River, NJ: Pearson.

Kwolek-Folland, A. (2001). Gender and business history. *Enterprise and Society, 2*(1), 1–10.

Kwolek-Folland, A. (2007). Gender, the service sector, and U.S. business history. *Business History Review, 81*(3), 429–450.

Leedy, P. D., & Ormrod, J. E. (2010). *Practical research: Planning and design* (9th ed.). Upper Saddle River, NJ: Prentice Hall.

Lynch, K. (2007). Modeling role enactment: Linking role theory and social cognition. *Journal for the Theory of Social Behaviour, 37*(4), 379–399. doi:10.1111/j.1468 -5914.2007.00349.x

Made in PA, (2011-2012). Industry pulse. Made in PA. Retrieved from http://content.yudu.com/Library/A1zujj/MadeinPAmagazine Fall/resources/index.htm

Mathur, S., & Chadha, N. K. (2010). The glass ceiling: Exploring the skewed dynamics of myths, realities, and changing landscapes. *Learning Community: An International Journal of Education and Social Development, 1*(2), 167–172.

McCrimmon, M. (2012). The future of leadership. Retrieved from http://www.leadersdirect.com/the-future-of-leadership

McQueen, L., & Zimmerman, L. (2006). Using the interpretive narrative research method in interdisciplinary research projects. *Journal of Nursing Education, 45*(11), 475–478.

Moustakas, C. (1994). Phenomenological research methods. Thousand Oaks, CA: Sage.

Musteen, M., Baker, V. L., & Baetan, V. L. (2006). CEO attributes associated with a attitude toward changes: The direct and moderating effect of CEO tenure. *Journal of Business Research,* (59), 604–612.

Neuman, W. L. (2005). Social research methods: Qualitative and quantitative approaches (6th ed.). Boston, MA: Allyn & Bacon.

Okafor, C., & Amalu, R. (2010). Entrepreneurial motivations as determinants of women entrepreneurship challenges. *Petroleum Gas University of Ploiesti Bulletin, Economic Sciences Series, 62*(2), 67–77.

organizational citizens' behavior across cultures. *Journal of Organizational Behavior, 28,* 1035–1057.

Pârlea-Buzatu, D. (2011). The social psychology of work: Career development of professional women. *Contemporary Readings in Law and Social Justice, 2*(2), 331–336.

PGH Business News. (2012). Pittsburgh business news. Retrieved from http://www.bizjournals.com/pittsburgh/news/

Pittsburgh Businesstimes. (2010). Pittsburgh's Top 7: Pittsburgh-area women-owned

businesses. Retrieved from http://www.bizjournals.com/pittsburgh/news/2010/10/22/top-7-women-owned-businesses.html

Pittsburgh Businesstimes. (2010). Pittsburgh Book of lists. Top 7: Pittsburgh-area women-owned businesses. Retrieved from http://www.bizjournals.com/pittsburgh/news/2010/10/22/top-7-women-owned-businesses.html

PittBusiness. (2011). PittBusiness_University of PGH: Leadership. Retrieved from http://www.cba.pitt.edu/

Pittsburgh Technology Council. (2012). News and publication Pittsburgh region. Regional and

Global News & Publications - Pittsburgh Tech Council. Retrieved from http://www.pghtech.org/news-and-publications/

Presencing Institute. (2012). Theory U: Presencing. Retrieved from http://www.presencing.com/docs/publications/execsums/Theory_U_2pageOverview.pdf

Rose, A. M. (1951). The adequacy of women's expectations for adult roles. *Social Forces*, 30(1), 69–77.

Santovec, M. L. (2010). Women's metaphor: From "glass ceiling" to "labyrinth." *Women in Higher Education, 19*(12), 1–2.

Sapolsky, R. M. (2004). *Why zebras don't get ulcers* (3rd ed.) New York, NY: Owl Books.

Savage-Austin, A. R., & Honeycutt, A. (2011). Servant leadership: A phenomenological study of practices, experiences, organizational effectiveness, and barriers. *Journal of Business and Economics Research, 9*(1), 49–54. Retrieved from http://journals.cluteonline.com/index.php/JBER/article/view/939/923

Scharmer, C. O. (2009). *Theory U: Leading from the future as it emerges.* San Francisco, CA: Berrett-Koehler.

Seidman, S. (2004). *Contested knowledge: Social theory today* (3rd ed.). Malden, MA: Blackwell.

Shambaugh, R. (2007). It's not a glass ceiling, it's a sticky floor: Free yourself from the hidden behaviors sabotaging your career success assumptions. McGraw-Hill Publishers

Shank, G. D. (2006). *Qualitative research: A personal skills approach* (2nd ed.). Upper Saddle River, NJ: Pearson.

Turner, R.H. (1962). Role taking: Process versus conformity. In A. Rose (Ed.), *Human behavior and social processes* (pp. 20–40). Boston, MA: Houghton-Mifflin.

U.S. Department of Labor, Bureau of Labor Statistics, (2009). *Women in the labor force: A databook.* Washington, DC: Author.

U.S. Department of Labor, Bureau of Labor Statistics. (2010, August 6). The employment Situation—July 2010. Washington, DC: Author.

Van Emmerik, H. C. (2010). Gender ratio, societal culture, and male and female leadership. *Journal of Occupational and Organizational Psychology, 83*(4), 895.

Wolfram, H., Mohr, G., & Schyns, B. (2006). Professional respect for female and male leaders: Influential gender-relevant factors. *Women in Management Review, 22*(1), 19–32.

Yoder, J. D. (2008). What every woman should know about the gendered maze of becoming a leader. *Psychology of Women Quarterly, 32*(4), 490–491. doi:10.1111/j.1471-6402.2008.00460_7.x.

Yukl, G. (2010). *Leadership in organizations* (7th ed.). Upper Saddle River, NJ. Pearson.

Yukl, G., & Lepsinger, R. (2005). Why integrating the leading and managing roles is essential for organizational effectiveness. *Organizational Dynamics, 34*(4), 361–375.

Zahidi, S., & Ibarra, H. (2010). *The corporate gender gap report.* Geneva, Switzerland: World Economic Forum. Retrieved from https://members.weforum.org/pdf/gendergap/corporate2010.pdf

www.ingramcontent.com/pod-product-compliance
Lightning Source LLC
Chambersburg PA
CBHW051726170526
45167CB00002B/821